About the Author

Marisette Edwards van-Linden van den Heuvell was born in the Netherlands and is currently a Pittsburgh-based software engineer who has managed to survive 30 years longer than nature apparently intended. Today, Marisette is an avid rower, competing nationally. She is the mother of two sons, her pride and joy. Marisette's love of writing is inspired by her vivid memories and in-depth research of life and family. In her own words, "Such information seems too interesting to keep to myself."

Dedication

This book is dedicated to the memory of my parents, Jan and Marijke van Linden van den Heuvell, without whose influence, love, and support I doubt I would have had the strength, courage, and wisdom to endure the challenges thrown at me by life.

Marisette Edwards-van Linden van
den Heuvell

TIGER IN THE DARK

AUSTIN MACAULEY
PUBLISHERS LTD.

A CIP catalogue record for this title is available from the British Library.

ISBN 9781786295941 (Paperback)
ISBN 9781786295958 (Hardback)
ISBN 9781786295965 (E-Book)

www.austinmacauley.com

First Published (2016)
Austin Macauley Publishers Ltd.
25 Canada Square
Canary Wharf
London
E14 5LQ

Acknowledgments

I had the extraordinary good fortune to be raised by two people who overcame their own difficulties to create a supportive, loving, and adventurous nuclear family. Because my parents were so loving and committed to each other and their children, I had the resources I needed to cope with the challenges of illness and loss that I endured. Mom, Dad, my brother Hugo, and my sister Nicolette were the foundation of love and support that I leaned upon. My maternal grandmother "Oma" was also an enormous influence on my life. She lived to be nearly 102, giving me quite a high bar to aspire to. My husband Dave was the rock I clung to.

My friends provided love and support in too many ways to count. Over the decades we may have been separated by miles or busy lives, but the connection built by our common experience remains strong. My best friend Sue Ayre and her husband Rick are across the country now, but I know I need only to call and Sue will be there for me. My other friends will recognize themselves in the body of the book. They all helped me cope – or just to feel normal when that was what I needed,

My sons Ian and Erik blessed my life and have grown into amazing and wonderful young men. I consider them my very own cheering section. Erik and his childhood friend Dave Gerardi both joined the military and I want to take this opportunity to say how inspired and grateful I am that these young people voluntarily step up to serve their country, in spite of the great potential risk to their own lives. The dedication of these people gives me hope for the future.

Lori Wippel, who once was my children's nanny, spent months typing the first draft of this manuscript on top of taking care of the boys. She helped me overcome the first hurdle of "no time to write" while I worked and raised children.

Dr. Rand Himes literally saved my life. When the health maintenance organization responsible for my care delayed treatment, he went to great lengths to overcome the bureaucracy and ensure that I immediately received the specialty care that I needed. I am deeply grateful for his dedication to his patients. He is what a doctor should be.

My friend and neighbor Nancy ("Nini") Schultz offered in such an encouraging way to read the manuscript that my hesitation to let anyone see it was overcome. She kindly made improvement suggestions that were so on target that I ended up incorporating them with ease.

Dad's wife Joanne was dedicated to keeping him home at the end of his long illness. In the course of his illness we became fast friends, through daily phone calls that we continue to make since his death. Her support means the world to me.

Finally, my mentor Andrew Jobling inspired me to dust off the manuscript and then, with his incessantly positive attitude, dragged me kicking, screaming, and whining over and around all the obstacles I put in my own way.

Without him I probably would not have gotten to the point of publication. Thank you!

The year 1985 is drawing to a close. I am 25 and pregnant with my first child, and something just feels wrong.

Since I was 12 years old, I've held two deep beliefs: I want to have children, and I don't expect to live to see my 30th birthday. Being pregnant at 25 creates an unfathomable tension between those two beliefs, which seems completely illogical yet keeps me in a constant state of internal dread.

On the outside, I am leading a normal life. My husband, Dave[1], and I are in the final stages of buying our first house and preparing to move to it. He is working as a remodeling contractor and I am working as a software engineer. I have been taking care of myself, going to the doctor for regular prenatal checkups, eating right, and going to aerobics classes regularly. Both of our parents live nearby and are supportive and excited about their coming first grand-child.

On the inside, I have been having this feeling of impending doom that I haven't really shared with anyone. I desperately want my baby, but I am sure being a mother will ruin my career. I am terrified something will happen to my baby and I'm convinced that I would be suicidal should I lose it. I am afraid to plan for the baby's arrival. It seems completely irrational and I am at a loss to understand my own morose outlook.

---

[1] Some names have been changed to protect privacy.

I have been dealing with pain in my shoulder for a few months now. I have trouble operating the gear shift of my car with my right arm, and using the computer mouse is making the back of my shoulder ache. There should be nothing to be concerned about, though – Dr. Macintyre, my family doctor, examined my shoulder and referred me to a physical therapist after concluding that I might have some tendinitis.

Between physical therapy sessions, I have been continuing with my aerobics classes in spite of the ache in my shoulder, since nothing has been found to suggest I shouldn't use it. During one aerobics class recently, we had our arms stretched out and were turning our hands palm up, then palm down, repeatedly. This really hurt my shoulder. I looked down at my right arm with my palm up and it looked misshapen. I thought to myself, "That explains the pain! My shoulder is out of joint." Who in their right mind thinks such a thing and then doesn't check up on this theory in the locker room, or at home, or with the treating physician? Someone in denial is who.

For advice I have been depending a lot on my friends Leslee and Barb, who I met at my first job out of college. They have been my mentors getting started in my engineering career, and we have remained friends since I moved on to my current job. When they attended my wedding, they had each recently had their first baby (Leslee's baby was actually the youngest person at our wedding). So they are a valuable resource to turn to with questions about balancing marriage, babies, and an engineering career.

Barb's baby was born unexpectedly prematurely. Sometime after the discovery of the "dislocated shoulder" set my mind at ease, Barb and I were talking on the phone about my latest checkup. She told me that, now that I am nearly 24 weeks along, the baby is viable and could survive if born early.

The next morning in the shower I found the lump.

It was in the front of my arm near the underarm, so it was only visible with my arm raised. The pain was radiating to the top and back of the shoulder; no one looked in the front. It was like there was a golf ball half-buried in my biceps tendon – roughly that size and shape, but smooth. It was hard and didn't move around if I pushed on it – which I did, over and over, but every time it was still there.

Dread hit me with full force. I felt cold, prickly sweat as I examined this ugly thing. I showed it to Dave, and some other people at work. Everyone agreed this was strange. As soon as the doctor's office opened, I was on the phone asking for an appointment. The wait for the next day was agonizing. I was terrified.

My appointment was with Dr. Himes, my obstetrician. When he examined the lump, he told me he thought it was just a cyst. I had a 99.9% chance that it was benign. I felt reassured and relaxed for the first time since I found the lump. We discussed how to handle this in light of my pregnancy. There doesn't seem to be any rush to remove it, but since it has been causing me pain for months, I thought it would be best to get it removed before I start carrying around a newborn. Dr. Himes confirmed that, as long as I had the surgery under local anesthetic, there would be minimal risk to the baby.

Surgery was arranged within a week, to be done by a general surgeon, Dr. Fisher. I was awake and felt the baby doing somersaults inside me while I lay on the operating table. Dr. Fisher kept up the chatter as he sliced a 3" incision on the front of my arm right below the underarm, from front to back. I felt no pain, but I did feel pressure as he spread my muscle to dig this thing out. He had to work pretty hard at it. I started out as a pre-med student and volunteered as an Emergency Medical Technician. So I was interested in what was going on. I glanced down to see my arm opened up and a 1/4" layer of fat visible above the red muscle. It gave me incentive to lose weight after I have the baby. He finally pulled the cyst free and showed it to me. It looked like a golf ball-sized piece of meat in a see-through sack of skin. Looking at that made me want to become a vegetarian right then and there.

Dr. Fisher confirmed what Dr. Himes told me – this looks like a benign cyst. But just to be sure, he sent it down to the pathology lab. He stitched up the wound, congratulated me on doing so well during the surgery, and promised to call me with the results of the pathology report.

2:30 p.m.

Dr. Fisher called me at 11:30 today. I was sleeping on the couch because I hadn't slept well at night. Yesterday, I had a lump in my upper right arm, next to my underarm, removed under local anesthesia because I'm 24 weeks pregnant and general anesthesia would affect the baby. The lump was the size of a golf ball. It was fascinating and scary to see such a thing come out of me – it was in a sack and it seemed to be graded from dark red on the bottom to lighter in the middle to fatty, lumpy yellow tissue on the top. I looked at my arm when the lump was out but my arm was still open and I could see a good 1/4" of lumpy yellow stuff. I thought at the time that it really was ugly and as soon as the baby was born I was going to get rid of it.

I wasn't worried at all. The only reason I didn't go to work was that I didn't want to contrive a plastic bag over the bandage to take a shower. It hurt, too, so I just wanted to stay home and catch up on my sleep. When Dr. Fisher called the worrying started. He said the pathologist had found some suspicious fibers and that I would need "further treatment". He said he had talked to my family doctor, Dr. Macintyre, and that she would refer me to an oncologist.

I knew that meant a cancer doctor – I burst into tears. It must be hard for doctors to give that sort of news. I hung up and tried to reach Dave, who was painting at the house of friends of ours, Marko and Terri (Terri is also my project lead at work), but after 25 rings he still didn't answer. Then I noticed that I had Marko's work number in my address book, and remembered that he lived close enough to walk to work. I called him and asked him to go home and ask Dave to call me.

While I was waiting for Dave to call, I called Dr. Macintyre's office and was told she'd call back. I cried on the couch and waited. Dave called me and told me to hold on, he'd be right home. I cried as I told him, "Drive carefully – I need you in one piece right now."

At around 12:30 Dr. Macintyre called me back and said it was cancer – sarcoma – that attaches to muscle. She said she was consulting with Dr. Johnson, the oncologist engaged to treat the cancer, and the pathologist, and she hadn't gotten everything worked out yet. It was pretty certain that I would have to be operated on again to remove any other cancerous pieces left behind in the first surgery, and I would need radiation therapy, but no chemotherapy. Then she said they might have to get the baby out early. She had already talked to Dr. Himes, my obstetrician.

I started crying again and turned off the soup I'd just put on the stove. How could I be hungry at a time like this? But I was – the baby still had to be nourished.

Then she calmed me down by explaining that "early" wouldn't mean prematurely, just as soon as tests showed its lungs to be developed – around 36 weeks (12 weeks from now). When the lungs are developed a baby is no longer considered premature. We talked some more and she said she'd call back later.

Dave came home 5 minutes later and I told him everything. I didn't want to try to call Mom and Dad because I knew they were still en-route to Holland for their vacation at that exact time. I thought it would ruin their vacation. We talked about how we felt. Basically we're in shock but still optimistic. After all, I saw the tumor and it looked self-contained.

Dr. Macintyre called again while I was starting to write this. This time it sounded much better. Dr. Fisher thought he "got the whole thing" out. The pathologist believed that it was low to medium grade, meaning that it was unlikely to have spread, and he seemed to think it was the original tumor – I guess they can tell whether it has originated somewhere else. The oncologist said that since Dr. Fisher thought he removed it all and it was self-contained, we didn't need to go in surgically again. And the radiologist said that the amount of radiation needed would be too high for the baby, so he wants to wait until the baby is born. So now the plan is to keep a close eye on it, give the baby a chance to choose its birth date, and while I'm in the hospital with the baby, they'll do the test to see if the cancer appears anywhere else, as well as start radiation therapy.

So now it's three to four months of waiting. To me, the activist, I think that is going to be very difficult. But at this point, the main objective is to get a healthy baby out and keep me as healthy as possible too. What a day it's been! But I wrote all this with the arm that was operated on yesterday, so obviously I'm not in such bad shape. Now to call and get an appointment with Dr. Macintyre.

7:30 p.m.

We decided we must call people to tell them. Only one person was home so far – Jeff, our friend who had a benign brain tumor. He was far worse off than I am and he got through it intact. He said worrying would do no good. He promised to look it up in the medical library at the University of Pittsburgh and give me some more information (he's a graduate student there). When I told him the lump was malignant, I got the same hot flash that I got when Dr. Fisher told me it was malignant this morning. Saying it brings it home. But we've been joking about it, too: "What do you say when you call people – Hi, how are you, I've got cancer!?"

There is no point in trying to contact Mom and Dad; they are traveling right now. I adore them, especially Mom. She is beautiful, with dark straight hair, hazel eyes, and olive skin. She is brilliant, sweet, warm, and caring. She achieved her Ph.D. in clinical psychology after all of us kids were in grade school, but she still found time to do things like take us to the zoo and on picnics. I remember helping her with her dissertation by cutting out sentences from her typewritten pages and moving them around where she wanted them. She has a way of putting everyone at ease, and asks questions in such a way that they are telling her their life stories before they realize it. She has a successful private practice but keeps it part time so she can enjoy life, like riding her horses, skiing, sailing, camping, traveling with Dad, and watching sunsets. She's so young looking that she often gets confused for my sister, and I look forward to having her around for a long time. Dad, with his salt and pepper hair and piercing blue eyes, is handsome, witty and smart. He has a bunch of patents in aluminum recycling. They are the coolest parents I know. They both speak fluent English but with the cutest Dutch accents (they can't say "th", turning it into "d" or "s" – we torture Mom by asking her to say "thistle"). They survived Nazi occupation as kids in the Netherlands in World War II. Dad was old enough to remember. He has told us some hair-raising stories. Some day I'm going to write a book about his experiences. Mom and Dad (or "Mam" and "Pap" as we call them) got married young, and decided to check out the rest of the world after Dad got his engineering degree. We left there when I was 6 years old, my brother Hugo was 5, and my sister Nicolette was a baby. Luckily Mom and Dad live close to me in a suburb of Pittsburgh, PA. I'm so glad I can just stop by and have tea with Mom. Hugo and I are only

14 months apart and once we stopped our sibling squabbling at around age 11-12, we've been best friends and we tell each other everything. He lives in New York and works for an airline. My "baby sister" Nicolette, 5-1/2 years younger, is going to college in Vermont. The rest of our relatives all live in the Netherlands, so Mom and Dad go back often. They just left last night for this visit.

Given that nobody could be reached, we both got busy packing books and glasses for the move to our first house, scheduled two weeks from today. It feels better to do something than to sit around getting morose. But we still have some talking and thinking to do. You can't assimilate it all in one day.

10:05 p.m.

Dave got a hold of his parents. Telling family is worse than hearing it yourself. His Mom started crying, put his Dad on the phone, and after Dave explained everything, it sounded like Dad was crying, too. I wish they wouldn't do that. It almost makes me feel like a jerk for causing the bad news. Terri, my project leader and friend, with whom I shared an apartment all last summer when we were working at a steel mill in Indiana, called to see how I was. Also, Marty and Laura, friends from college who live nearby, called to offer help whenever we need it (Jeff called them at my request). Marty's father died of cancer, and his mother has had it, too.

Hugo is the only one in my family that I could reach. Hugo didn't take it well either. He's flying to Holland tomorrow, so if I can't reach Mom and Dad, I guess he will be able to tell them. It's snowing and I think the lines to Vermont must be down, so I can't reach Nicolette. I can't wait until everyone knows and accepts it.

10:00 a.m.

With so many thoughts running through my head, it's hard to get them all down coherently. I'm alone at work right now, trying to make up for one of the days I took off for the operation. That's so I'll have time to take for the baby. I'm furious at my company right now, for putting me in the position that I can't take time off when I really need it because they don't offer short-term disability. What if things get worse and I have to take a month off? How will we pay the bills? I wish fervently that I hadn't left my first job because the "opportunities" looked better here! There I had unlimited sick days as well as short-term disability. If I had stayed, I would still have vacation days to take, instead of having to save them up to use as sick time. The next job change I make, I vow that I'll take less pay for better benefits. But at this point I can't do a thing about it. That's what makes me so angry in the first place. I really feel stuck! After the baby ...

Yesterday was a day of ups and downs (actually high lows and bottomless pit lows). I woke up at 4:30 a.m. and was pretty much wide awake after that, between discomfort and trying to decide what to tell people when

23

I go back to work. As soon as 6:00 a.m. came around, I got Dave up and got him to cut my bandage off. The scar looks really good (as far as scars go). I got in the shower. There is nothing like a morning shower after two days in bed! I felt so fresh and clean (not sick, cancerous, at all).

As soon as I got dressed with Dave's help, I ran downstairs and called Oma, my grandmother in Holland. I was hoping Mom and Dad would already be there, but they were still on their way from the airport to her house. I asked Oma to have them call me. I hated not telling her what was up, but I don't have enough command of the Dutch language to be able to explain it. Besides, I thought Mom and Dad could explain the entire story once I'd talked to them. So Dave and I had breakfast and he drove me to work. It was a silent ride. I was lost in my own world. When I got to work, I told my office-mate Max (I gave her that nickname based on her last name – she was the next new person after I arrived and we get along really well). After that it became easier to choose the words to say to other people. Everyone was basically very supportive and kind. I may hate the company policies, but I love the people.

Dad called me at work from Holland at about 8:30 a.m. We talked for about 20 minutes. He was already prepared, since I'd told them after the operation that I would only call them in Holland if it was bad news. He was very supportive and loving and optimistic that everything would turn out all right. I told him that everything that could be done, was being done, and so there was nothing we all could do but wait, and they might as well enjoy their vacation. I told him that I didn't want to call them with bad news, but I remembered how mad I was years ago, when Hugo and I were in Holland for the summer, that they hadn't called to let us know our dog died after being hit by a car. We were so shocked when we came home and life had changed unexpectedly. So I knew they'd feel the same way being left out of something important happening here, even if they couldn't do anything. He said he wouldn't want it any other way. I almost started crying when I said it was malignant (again the hot flash), but I got a hold of myself – an international phone call is no place to waste time crying. I talked to Mom for a minute too. She wants to use her clinical psychology training to help me, by hypnotizing me and helping me to imagine my immune cells attacking the cancer cells to try to speed up the healing. I said that I'd already decided I wanted to do that and we could start as soon as she got home. She'll be here for one night between Holland and her conference in Phoenix, so I asked her to come stay with us that night. She said she would. Everyone wished me strength (*sterkte* in Dutch) and promised to bring back my favorite goodies from Holland. After we hung up I felt much better. Now I still have to get a hold of Nicolette.

The rest of the day went fairly well until Terri came in and said she was leaving Mark in charge while she's away next week. I got really furious (inside) because I've been working on this project for six months and Mark, my peer, was only assigned to it a week ago. Of course it makes sense from the point of view that I'm going to be gone myself part of Tuesday and all day Friday for the closing and doctor's appointments, but I was in the mood to feel discriminated against. Between getting less responsibility on the project overall because I'm going to have a baby, and not even getting to be temporary project leader because I had to go to so many doctors because of CANCER, I really started to feel sorry for myself.

To backtrack a little, Dr. Macintyre called me at around 10:00 a.m. on Friday and told me that she and Dr. Himes had decided together that I should see a specialist at Magee-Women's Hospital who saw a lot of pregnant women with cancer. His name is Scott Williams (which amused me because we have a somewhat wild and crazy friend with the same name). Dr. Williams had a time slot open for Tuesday, so I only have to wait a few more days to talk to someone who can tell me more about what I have. I was supposed to call North Hills Passavant Hospital to get the pathologist's report and slides, but they wouldn't let me have them – they'd rather trust the U.S. mail! I think I have just a tad more interest in getting them there than the U.S. mail does! That's what Dr. Williams's secretary thought, too, but she couldn't convince them either. So we set up a double check between us to make sure they receive everything since Dr. Williams HAS to have the slides before he can tell me anything.

Dave called me in the morning just to see how I was. He is such a wonderful husband! Without him, I'd be lost right now. But he keeps me steady. I love him so much!

I worked late yesterday, again to make up time. Everyone else left except Rich, our resident computer wizard, and Carol, the cleaning lady. I started feeling really lonely and morose and I couldn't leave until Dave got there. Carol came in to talk to me. She wanted to know why I was still there, and I told her it was because I was waiting for Dave. She asked if we only had one car, and I said, "No, I just can't drive because of the operation." She said, "Oh, yes, how did that turn out?" I got really down and said, "Not good." She said that she'd also been operated on for cancer, two times, and she was fine now. She figured it would come back again, too, but that she'd get it taken care of again. She said worrying doesn't do a thing for you. She also said she was sure everyone had cancer in his body and God knows what triggers it. Dave arrived just then and she gave me words of encouragement and a big hug and kiss. That was good, to talk to someone who had been through it.

I told Dave that I was depressed and wanted a present. So we went to a maternity store where I've gotten friendly with the owner. I couldn't feel too sad in front of her because her little seven-year-old daughter has Cystic Fibrosis and there's no cure for that. I got a nice big red vest that I'm wearing now. It makes me feel less big and clunky since it is so loose on me.

There wasn't any food in the house, so Dave and I went to a little local restaurant. I was still feeling down and Dave was trying to tell me that there were a lot of worse things it could be. I realized that it wasn't so much being afraid of dying that had me upset, because I really believe that this is going to be cured. It's the idea of something growing within me that is not a natural working part of me, but something capable of killing me unless I fight it. And I can't fight it by myself. I need help, technology and doctors to do it. Plus, it has been doing this to me without my knowledge and I have no control over it. My own body is betraying me. I've lost trust in my feeling of well-being; that feeling could be hiding something dangerous, even if I have no indication of anything being wrong. After explaining all of that to Dave, I felt much better. Not that it solved anything, but just realizing and expressing my self-doubt helped me deal with it.

Now that I've written all of this down, I can get to work again. One positive thing is that my arm feels really good. I haven't taken Tylenol for two days now, and my range of motion keeps getting better. Every indication of good health, wouldn't you say?

9:00 a.m.

Evenings seem to be the most difficult – most of my doubts seem to surface then. Last night I felt a twinge in my leg and another in my lung and I got scared that it had already spread. And there are no guarantees that it hasn't – after all, it was 99.9% sure that my tumor was benign; how sure can I be now that it hasn't spread? It began to overwhelm me last night, but luckily I have Dave's shoulder to cry on and his positive attitude to keep me up. I guess I knew that the first day's relief would not last for long, but I had hoped that I would be stronger somehow. Dave tells me I'm brave, but I'm not so sure. I do wish Mom and Dad were home already – I could use their support. When I was talking to Sue the other day about my tumor I was telling her about my conversation with my parents and I suddenly felt so sad for her because she doesn't have parents anymore. She's been my best friend ever since we were both the new kids in High School. Her dad killed himself about a year before we met. Her mother was left to raise six children on her own. Then the unthinkable happened: two weeks before my wedding, when we were 24, Sue's mom was on a business trip in Maryland, crossing the street in broad daylight, and a truck turning into the intersection struck her with its side mirror. Her head hit the pavement and she never regained consciousness. All this played through my head as I told Sue how much I needed my Mom home, and I could just feel Sue thinking, "If this would happen to me, I couldn't talk to my mother." There has been so much tragedy in our group of friends over the past few years. Why do we have to be tested again and again? And why does it have to happen to me when I should be the happiest, waiting for our first baby? Then I feel guilty about feeling sorry for myself like this because it's not as serious as other people's troubles, like the friend of our receptionist who found out she had leukemia when she was pregnant and had to go in isolation in Ohio to be treated – away from husband and brand new baby. When I heard about that (it was before I found my lump) I thought how hard that would be to deal with. But then, I can't be sure I won't have the same situation in April. I hope that I can stay with Dave and the baby; that is one thing I <u>could not </u>do is live without Dave.

So I'm thankful that I have Dave, my family, his family and all our friends, and that I at least feel healthy. I talked to the lady who owns the maternity store yesterday and she was also very positive. It seems like the people who deal with illness successfully all develop a positive outlook and try to take each day as it comes and appreciate the beauties they find in it.

I called Dave's parents yesterday to make sure they were all right and to see if they wanted us to stop over in the evening. They already had plans but they seemed relieved to talk to me and hear me sounding healthy and optimistic. I put up a good front sometimes – other times I really do feel optimistic. Dave's mother is already rallying to her old self – the eternal optimist! We may go see them today if Dave gets done early enough. He's working again today – he's been working so hard so he could be with me when I needed him! One question raised was what to tell his grandparents. I don't think it's fair to tell them over the phone; I think it's important that they see me looking calm and healthy. I think that does more <u>for</u> people than the news does <u>to</u> them. It seems like the people at work who saw me were much less upset than the people who only heard about it. One good example is Dan, my boss, who heard just before he came home for the weekend (he's in Chicago for a field installation until God knows when): Dan came in yesterday afternoon when I was still there and told me that he had heard already. Then he said he hadn't expected me to be there, and that he had expected me to <u>be different.</u> I think he meant that he expected me to appear haggard, overwhelmed or tired, and to be negative or upset or crying. After we talked for a while he seemed to be much more comfortable being with me. Anyway, the whole point is that people are less shocked if I can tell them in person so they don't get visions of me as an AIDS victim on death row.

Unfortunately, I can't do that with Nicolette, so I hope I can somehow communicate my sameness to her over the phone. I still haven't been able to reach her.

We got a letter from Dave's Dad yesterday:

12-6-85

David,

We have a new Chinese restaurant in Coraopolis that gives you an education with the placemat. You were born under the sign of the tiger, and you are sincere, sensitive and courageous. You displayed all of that in our telephone conversation last night.

Your mother and I were emotional because we think of Marisette as our daughter, and this should be a time of joy becoming a mother and a father. This should be a time of sunshine not of dark clouds.

You two have a sensible approach to your problem, and to have taken the steps you have seems to be as timely as possible.

You will now be "Tiger" instead of "Sport" in my everyday thoughts. We are proud of both of you in your acceptance of the facts and you are in our prayers daily—

Dad

Another blessing – we are loved!

9:00 a.m.

Since Nicolette is the youngest and always had trouble with school, requiring a majority of Mom's time and attention to get through her homework, it was a bit surprising that she decided to go to college so far from home. With nearly six years in age difference, I still tend to think of her as the baby. I finally got through to her in Vermont, and Nicolette took it better than anyone else so far – probably because I downplayed it a little, although I gave her the facts over the entire conversation. I just didn't hit her with "I've got cancer" right away. She asked casually if there was any other incidence of cancer in the family, so I know that she's aware of what I was talking about.

Dave worked all day yesterday and still didn't get done completely, poor thing. Today he starts painting at Leslee and Mike's house. So he'll have to finish this job next week. He really bears up well in a crisis – he's been my saving grace. He's funny, too – very overprotective – he won't let me carry anything with my right arm and he makes sure I get enough sleep. Our relationship seems even more special than ever since we're going through this together.

We went to Sue's house for dinner last night. It was nice and relaxed and a good dinner. I feel more like my own old self again.

At Sue's house Dave tried their rowing machine and now he wants one, too. It's about time – I've been trying to talk him into one for years.

Mom is coming home tonight! Hooray! I can dump on her (just kidding).

4:20 p.m.

It just struck me as funny, looking at my calendar – I scheduled haircuts for both of us on the same day we're going to see the cancer specialist, since we're going to be in the right part of town anyway. Drama and mundanity go side by side in real life.

I spent all morning making moving arrangements. I think it's great to have such a major distraction available. It gives me less time to brood.

This is the third day in a row that I have my red vest on (over different clothes each day – it's so versatile!). I think it's becoming my security blanket. Well, at least my favorite item of clothing.

Kathy, our secretary, went home early today. She just found out she was pregnant last week and she was spotting today. I hope she's okay. I remember how nervous I was until I was past 12 weeks, and how attached I already was to the baby. We talked about the theory that if a miscarriage should happen now, it would be because the baby was deformed, but I'm sure that won't make her feel a lot better if it happens. I'm keeping my fingers crossed for her.

Carol, the cleaning lady, just told me that her dad "put my name in at church". I guess that means somebody's praying for me. Isn't that nice? And her mother wanted to say hello to me. People are so nice!

Tuesday, December 10, 1985

Pregnancy 24 weeks, 3 days

A.D. 5 days

8:30 a.m.

Today we're going to the specialist, at 4:00 p.m. I'm very anxious about it.

Mom spent the night last night. We went to bed at around midnight and she woke up at 4:00 a.m. She said she must have been getting used to Holland time. Now she's going another 4 hours west, so she probably won't be able to sleep at all anymore. Mom was happy to be home to talk to me. She seemed to be about a day or two behind in the acceptance process. She was saying "It's not fair!" and "How could such a thing grow in your body? You're so young and healthy!" While in Holland, Mom and Dad went to see Jan Schoornagel, the oncologist they became friends with when Dolf, Dad's best friend, was dying of cancer of the colon. They were pretty rushed and the kids kept coming in and out of the room, but they did talk about it a little bit. Jan said that this would spread through the blood stream to the lungs but that it sounded good that it seemed to be self-contained. He said he couldn't say much more since he didn't know what grade it was, but he couldn't see why they couldn't radiate just the arm and shield the baby to make sure they killed whatever was left. It sounded just like everything I'd been told so far, and that's quite a relief. Contradictions from physicians would make it that much more difficult to deal with the situation.

He did say that with something this serious I should definitely get a second opinion. He preferred the doctors that work for Pitt at Presby (Presbyterian Hospital); he's heard a lot of good things about them. I'm hoping that Dr. Williams is one of those, because I'm so tired of going to doctors that I really balk at the idea of going to another doctor. But since Dr. Williams is not a regular consultant to the group my doctors belong to, I hope he can count as the second opinion. After all, he's making his own diagnosis from the slides, not going by the pathologist's report.

Since I've been hearing so much about it spreading to the lungs, I've been feeling pains in the left lung – on the front lower lobe and between my sixth and eighth (?) ribs in the back. It feels like muscle tension, but that's what my shoulder felt like, too. Also, I have a definite painful spot in my upper right thigh towards the back I keep thinking "but it <u>couldn't</u> have spread" and then I remember how my arm started hurting – like a tired muscle – and that nobody expected it to be cancer, so if nobody expects it to have spread, how can I be so sure?

Today my arm is sore again – I don't think driving is very good for it – or typing either. Too bad I can't take time off. But I guess I'll live with my benefits as they are for the time being – at least I have enough to provide me with <u>some</u> financial security over the long run (this is Mom's influence speaking).

Dad comes home on Saturday – I can't wait to have them both close again.

Mom called Nicolette last night and it turns out my sister was more worried about me than she seemed to be at first. She sounded like she had thought about it a lot. Luckily she has her boyfriend Danny there to talk to. I knew she'd be upset when she connected it with her best friend Lisa's mother, who found out she had leukemia and died within a year.

She knew also that Opa, Dad's father, died of leukemia. I didn't even know that! He was in his early seventies and had no symptoms until three weeks before he died. He had the airplane tickets to come visit us in Tennessee and he never got to use them. I hope I'm luckier than that.

For some reason, all of my life I've been sure that I was going to have to deal with a terrible disease. I also believed that I wasn't going to live past 30. I don't know why I started believing that as a youngster, but I hope to God that I was wrong! I always tried to live my life so that I would have nothing to be sorry for if I would die or lose my health. I have succeeded – if I died today I would die happy. But I don't want to die. I don't want to leave Dave and my friends and family. I want to live until I'm Oma's age. If I kick this cancer, then I will have licked the disease I've been waiting for since I was a child. I have to do it – I hope this pain in my back is just a sore muscle!

Jan also said that Mom's hypnosis idea was a good one – even if it doesn't do anything, it will help keep me calm and give me a feeling of control. But it should be used to augment, not substitute for medical treatment.

Carol explained to me that the entire church would be praying for me. If that doesn't do it, I don't know what will!

I don't know if I can make it till 4:00 p.m.

10:00 a.m.

Today is one of those days that I sit at my desk trying to think and the only thing that comes out is, "I have cancer. My tumor was malignant. I have cancer ..." it must be anxiety about going to the specialist. I guess I feel like it's dangerous to expect good news because the last time I did that I got knocked off my feet.

I just talked to the receptionist about her friend Marlene. Her baby is six months old and she has to go to Ohio next week for the bone marrow transplant. Then she has to be in isolation for <u>6 months!</u> What agony! Her husband is allowed to see her but she can only see her baby behind glass. She has leukemia. I hope somebody's praying for her – she needs it more than I do.

Mom was going to call me before she left for Phoenix to tell me who Dr. Schneiderman suggested I see (he's an acquaintance through her work and Jan knew his name and suggested asking him) I guess she didn't get a hold of him; she's on her way to Phoenix now.

Wednesday, December 11, 1985

Pregnancy 24 weeks, 4 days

A.D. 6 days

9:45 a.m.

Well, here goes. It was good that I was expecting bad news yesterday because that's just about all we got. Dr. Williams explained several things (he was very good at that). There are three types of cancer. One attacks the vital organs, the second attacks the blood-producing organs (leukemia), and the third, sarcoma, attacks the connective tissues – tendons, muscles, cartilage, etc. That's what I have. To compare the rarity of my cancer, he mentioned that 130,000 cases of breast cancer turn up every year, while 7,000 cases of this turn up. So the 99.9% chance of it being benign was more than accurate.

He said that there were several factors used to gauge the seriousness of the tumor – grade, size and location. Grade is determined by how many cells are in the mitotic state (dividing, i.e. multiplying). If there are few, the grade is low and the tumor is called "indolent". This is the least serious. High grade means that many cells were dividing and the tumor was growing very rapidly. This is the most serious. He grades mine as medium, meaning there was enough multiplying to assume that it was growing fairly rapidly. He believes that it wasn't there for very long.

41

As far as size goes, something smaller than 5 cm is much more manageable, while greater than 5 cm is more serious. Mine was measured at 2 x 3 x 5 cm, so it's right on the border.

Location was the questionable part from his point of view. I told him that Dr. Fisher had spread apart the muscle to get at the tumor, and that he said it was between the muscle and the bone. But he didn't seem to believe my account, or at least he wanted to verify it with Dr. Fisher. Good policy, I guess, since I felt it but didn't see it. He asked if it hurt under local anesthesia, because the more it hurt, the deeper he went. I told him it hurt a lot when Dr. Fisher was spreading the muscle. Then he made a comment like, "But if you wince when I pull the tapes off our skin, maybe it didn't really hurt that much." I think it was a joke, but it made me mad. Sure I winced when he took the tapes off – the whole area was tender from surgery 6 days earlier. But I'm no baby and if I say something hurt a lot, it did! He made a comment that doctors often don't believe their patients' descriptions of pain, symptoms or lumps, but I seemed like an intelligent person and he believed me. I got the feeling that maybe he believed me more than usual, but still not everything. I'll show him to doubt me!

My kind of cancer is supposed to by asymptomatic – people just find the lump and never felt any pain. So he was surprised that I said I had so much pain in my shoulder. He thought it was unrelated. When I told him that my arm felt better as soon as the lump was out, he looked at me skeptically. That's when he made the comment about believing what patients say. If you strip away my reaction to his comment, though, the implication of <u>painless</u> tumors growing inside me is enormous. There is no way for me to know if there's another one anywhere else. It's interesting that I stopped feeling as many twinges everywhere after I heard that. I have to go for diagnostic tests, but I don't have to worry about every ache and pain.

Another problem with location is that the tumor was situated in a precarious spot in my body. It was sitting right where all the nerves to my hand run, where a major artery passes through, and where the biceps' and triceps' tendons attach to the bone. So it will be difficult to take out as much tissue as they normally like to, to ensure that they get most of the tumor.

After explaining all this to us, he outlined methods of treatment. He said radical surgery was still the first requirement, and due to the location that was going to be very difficult. He said that we want to maintain functionality, so they can't touch the nerves. He explained that with a breast or the top of the thigh or something, a lot of tissue could be removed without impairing functionality (implying that breasts' functions are not needed – I suppose that's true in relation to staying alive), but removing my dominant arm or severing nerves in it would impair functionality to an unacceptable degree. Whew! For a moment I thought he wanted to cut off my arm. But no, just a big chunk of it.

He said he had conferred with other doctors who advised immediate amputation, but he preferred to try to save the arm. He did warn us that if he was forced to cut the main nerve to my arm, I might end up wanting an amputation because I would have no control over it. It would be like when you wake up after sleeping on it wrong, and you can't feel it or move it without picking it up with the other hand. He had had a male patient who requested an amputation after having his arm flop around, get caught in doors, and generally get in the way. I specified that I would prefer to have a dead arm in a sling than no arm at all, and I wanted a chance to come to the amputation conclusion on my own rather than wake up with a surprise missing arm.

After surgery, radiation is required to kill any remaining cells that escape detection – a clump of 1000 cells can start a new tumor but is only the size of a pin head. Most clumps can't be detected by scan until they're about 1 cm in diameter, or about 100 million cells. That's why radiation is used.

Chemotherapy is used throughout the body and is very toxic. He didn't say much about it and I believe he is basically ruling it out for the time being.

Now the big obstacle to treatment is the baby. He said we're going to have to carefully pick a path between harm to the baby's health and harm to my health, He does not think that we can wait even 10 weeks to begin treatment. (Then the baby would be 35 weeks and would almost surely survive without complications.) He said we would have to consider priorities here. We told him that we had discussed them and decided that my life had to come first. I hate to say that as if it's an easy thing to decide, but what kind of life would Dave and the baby have if I died at the baby's expense? Or even if I had to go through major surgery right after its birth? I'm not writing off the baby, and I pray that we can get it out healthy, but we have to start facing the possibility that we may lose the baby. I wish I could just turn back the clock and not find it for another two months! Then the question would be moot. No decisions were made last night – Dr. Williams wants to confer with other people and do some more research He's going to call me today and go over the options he's going to offer and we'll have to make our decision then.

I put a lot of this down on paper mechanically and technically because I can't stand to get emotional about it. Last night I sobbed in Dave's arms and felt angry and sorry for myself, but I can't spend my day at work crying. If I think about my baby dying, that's what I do (like now) so I just can't afford to do it. I pray that there is an acceptable solution.

10:30 p.m.

These are my notes from the phone conversation with Dr. Williams:

"35 weeks not an option

"30 weeks 85% now – abortion – baby could live – lots of intensive care, "radiation therapist reluctant to do therapy on baby – shield abdomen, "surgery – chemotherapy general – potential of going into labor."

Obviously our choices are all morose. If we take the baby now it'll be an abortion but the baby might live and no one will let it die, so it could spend months in intensive care and live to be severely handicapped.

Waiting until 35 weeks is not an option in Dr. Williams' mind – he thinks it's too much of a risk to me. He said if this cancer would be left untreated, I would die from it. Apparently giving it 10 weeks gives it too much of a head start on us.

Taking the baby at 30 weeks gives it an 85% chance of survival.

General anesthesia has made some women go into labor.

The radiation therapist does not want to radiate me while I'm pregnant. Another radiologist is willing to try shielding the abdomen.

Dr. Williams wants to do more surgery, two weeks later start radiation therapy for 6 weeks, five days a week, and then do chemotherapy for six months. My hair will fall out and I will feel nauseated all the time and I will be at risk for infections. The surgery is to get out clumps of cells – sarcoma is a false capsule tumor, meaning that it looks like it's in its own capsule but really there are cells of it outside the capsule. Radiation only kills cells that are dividing so any clumps have to be gone already. Since radiation kills cells that are dividing, we have to let the skin heal sufficiently before starting it. Chemotherapy is basically a poison that kills all fast-growing cells. Hair grows fast, so does bone marrow, and the lining of the stomach. That explains the hair falling out and the nausea. The bone marrow produces the red and white blood cells, so under chemotherapy I'll be more susceptible to infections.

Chemotherapy can affect my fertility.

This is what the doctor told us. When we asked if we could wait just two weeks, till after Christmas, he said he wouldn't recommend it.

Now the ball is in our court. Not only may our baby die, but it may be our only chance at having one.

We want the baby to live, so we're going to give it as much chance as possible. We're going to opt for surgery next week (right before moving to the new house) and give the baby at least two and a half weeks. Then we'll start the radiation trying to shield the baby. When it's determined that the baby is at more risk from the radiation than from being on its own, we'll take it out and hope it's a fighter. This may be our only one – I hope it gets a better chance than we've been getting.

It's so sad. Mom called soon after the doctor but I only got halfway through telling her the options when the connection got really bad. She told me to try calling her, so I did but couldn't get through. She called back and said she was going to find another phone. The connection was really bad this time. It snowed in Phoenix!

Fifteen minutes later she called again and she was crying. She said if I was going to die then why bother with all the treatments, just get the baby out healthy so there would be a part of me left. She said she couldn't find a cab and started walking down the highway, the rain was coming down in sheets and the road was slick and shiny and she started crying and thinking how terrible it all was. She found a little gas station where they only spoke Spanish and even though she couldn't remember a word of it (we lived in Mexico for three years; she speaks it fluently) they understood and brought a phone out from under the counter.

When she was crying like that I did, too. I felt so sorry for her out there all alone having to deal with this. She needs Dad the same way I need Dave. I told her, "Mom, I'm not going to die." I had just gotten to the part about this killing me if it was left untreated when the connection got so bad. I told her that Dr. Williams wants to cure me so I can live a long happy life after this. And I told her that we had made the decision to treat me and hope that the baby was strong enough to withstand and survive. Hope is just not a strong enough word – it's more like wanting something so badly that your heart aches, but you have to let it happen on its own.

Mom calmed down and got optimistic again (of sorts). I told her to learn all she could about hypnotherapy, the subject of her psychology conference, so she could help me when she got back. Now I hope she made it back to her hotel all right. I tried to call her there but I couldn't get through. Damn, of all the times for it to snow in Phoenix for the first time in 50 years!

Dave's grandmother called before the doctor and Dave told her all he knew at the time. Finally that's over. Then his Mom called after mine did and Dave told her everything. This time she was strong: "We'll win this fight!" We're going over there tomorrow evening.

Dave's asleep out of exhaustion. I can't believe it hasn't even been a week since we found out!

One of the saddest things of all is that my breasts are leaking in preparation for a baby to feed. Even if the baby lives, the radiation and chemotherapy make it stupid to breastfeed. So now I have to wear nursing pads but I'll never get to use them for nursing. Could it possibly get worse than this?

Thursday, December 12, 1985

Pregnancy 24 weeks, 5 days

A.D. 1 week

9:00 a.m.

I'm sitting here in the unheated new house waiting for the gas man to come. I looked downstairs to see the new electrical box and there is none! And I can't leave to call anyone until the gas man comes. My writing looks funny because my thumb hurts and is swollen. I hope it's just swelling from the surgery – not something to do with the cancer. I'm sure if it were the cancer they'd lop it off without a second thought. Then I'd have to become a left hander.

I didn't get much sleep last night. I kept waking up and crying over the baby. This morning I got up to take a shower and started crying uncontrollably in the bathroom. I went back and lay in bed with Dave. If it was just me, I wouldn't be so worried. But to give the baby such a slim chance is just so unbelievably difficult. We don't really want the baby exposed to radiation every day – I think we're going to want the baby taken when the radiation starts. That should be 27-28 weeks' gestation. I know the baby's chances are really rotten, but what else can we do? Expose it to radiation, so it can develop leukemia? We have to find out more about radiation and fetuses.

3:00 p.m.

I feel much better now – the gas is on, the electricity is fixed and the check for the closing is in my purse. I also feel resolved in what we're going to do. Hopefully the baby will have enough time to grow between now and the time radiation starts.

I talked to Dr. Macintyre today and she seems to like our approach. She said all the costs are covered, including specialists and chemotherapy. She'll make sure that anyone who's treating me will feel comfortable with our decisions, and if not, she'll find another doctor who does.

Dr. Williams is supposed to call back today.

I got calls from Barb and Leslee today. Both offered help and support, but best of all they offered to pump extra breast milk and freeze it for the baby! A veritable milk bank! I'm really touched by that. I think I'll try to get some good milk out of me, too, but it's wonderful to have access to their milk, too. Barb was very optimistic, as always, and thinks the baby is going to make it. I can have all her preemie baby clothes. I hope I'll need them. The baby's moving around a lot – saying, "I'm strong"!

Friday, December 13, 1985

Pregnancy 24 weeks, 6 days

A.D. 1 week, 1 day

Friday, the thirteenth, a traditionally unlucky day

The closing went well today. We're home owners now. We're supposed to feel good about it, but the situation sort of takes the thrill out of it all. We couldn't get motivated to do anything tonight – it was snowing and the slush was turning into ice – not good weather for moving furniture.

We saw Dr. Himes and Dr. Macintyre today. They're good people. They suggested we visit the NICU[2] at Magee-Women's Hospital to get an idea of what we were in for. We had talked about doing that last night, so we were happy to hear the suggestion. Dr. Himes said he'd do the C-section whenever we decide it needs to be done. We're going to do a sonogram when I'm in the hospital. Also a chest X-ray to make sure there aren't any big lumps. That will make us feel better waiting (unless they're in there). I found a small lump on one of my ribs but it feels different from the one in my arm. I pointed it out to the doctors and they think it's not bad. Dr. Williams will look at it before the surgery. Dr. Himes made me feel good. He wanted to know if I minded that he sent me to Dr. Williams because he wanted me to know that he hadn't abandoned me but

---

[2] Neonatal Intensive Care Unit

was just trying to get me the best information possible. They both acted like they really cared and would stand by me. I don't know if they realize how important that is – one day I'll let them know.

Dr. Williams called tonight. He had already talked to my doctors and said he would schedule the surgery for next week, Wednesday or Thursday. That's good – we'll have time for some moving and Mom and Dad will be back. And the baby will have a couple more days. Every day counts. Dr. Macintyre said I'd be in the hospital for 3 days or so, but Dr. Williams didn't commit himself. I think he said he'd get me in the same day as the surgery, but never actually answered my question about how long I'd be in. I can't imagine why it would be for a long time.

I'm really interested in seeing the NICU. I expect the babies to be tiny and pitiful, but it will help prepare us for our ordeal.

The doctors kept telling us about the problems that preemies face and that there is a possibility that, if the baby lives, it could be brain damaged or have lung disease. If the sonogram looks good, though, we want that baby to have a chance to make it, and if there's a problem, we'll simply have to deal with it. We have to take it one step at a time.

Terri called from Florida last night to tell me not to worry about taking time off. That was nice of her.

Mom called. She said Dad might be on his way home tonight. I hope not – it's a terrible night to be traveling.

They were showing the airport looking bad on the news, plus it's a long drive home and all the roads are icy. I hope he will be okay.

Dave's Grandma called and I told her what was up. She didn't seem to flinch, even at the part about taking the baby so early. She's a strong lady – I know how she was looking forward to that first great-grandchild. Let's pray she'll get her great-grandchild. I told her she could help by praying for me and the baby and she said, "Of course!" We don't pray (in the formal sense), but we'll take all the support we can get.

The hardest thing to deal with now that my pregnancy is obvious is when people ask me when I'm due. Usually I say March 30 and they say, "Oh, good, you'll have a chance to settle in." That makes me want to cry – that's the way it should be, dammit!

One good thing – my thumb feels all better. I don't have to worry about it and I can write all I want.

Monday, December 16, 1985

Pregnancy 25 weeks, 2 days

A.D. 1 week, 4 days

10:30 a.m.

This whole weekend was so busy that I didn't get a chance to write at all. I didn't get a chance to think about it much either, so this morning it hit me like a ton of bricks again. The biggest thing gnawing at me is whether the baby can make it. As long as the baby is all right, I will be. But as Oma pointed out when she called yesterday, if the baby dies I will be really depressed and it will be that much more difficult to go through the treatments. So just to say that my life comes before the baby's is not valid. My life is part of the baby's and vice versa. We're too intertwined to separate us. I'm so afraid the baby will die and that I won't even want to go on. A lot of people have made it through babies dying but not too many with the knowledge that this could be the only one.

I'm hitting a denial stage. I don't want to go through this anymore. I was daydreaming that they wouldn't find any more in my arm and that they would find out that the hospital got my lump mixed up with someone else's, and then I could sue them (even though I don't believe in suing) and I wouldn't have to worry about money anymore either.

That's the other thing eating at me. I have to work to keep the insurance that pays for the treatments; I have three weeks of sick and vacation time left, and after that nothing. Those three weeks will be taken up just with the surgery. When I have a tiny baby at home who has to be fed every two hours, I'll be going through chemo and working. How will we manage it? I could go part time, but I think I'm going to be exhausted no matter what. If I wouldn't have to work at all I'd be exhausted. Terri suggested that I work from home, so I can do that at least. But I just don't know how I'm going to handle it all.

Tuesday, December 17, 1985

Pregnancy 25 weeks, 3 days

A.D. 1 week, 5 days

2:15 p.m.

I'm at the new house right now. I have to leave in about 15 minutes to go talk to Dr. Germaine, the radiation therapist. Dave can't come with me. He's trying really hard to get all his work done so he can concentrate on me and the new house.

It's snowing now, so I'll probably have to deal with murderous traffic.

Thursday morning at 7:00 a.m. I have to be at Magee-Women's Hospital for surgery. I should get out on Friday, though, so I should be able to direct traffic for the move. I'm nervous about the surgery. I don't know how much disability to expect from my arm. I expect it will hurt more and longer, but if he's cutting out a lot of muscle, will I be able to use it normally soon? I hate being dependent on other people.

I talked to Dr. Williams yesterday. I started to ask him about the chemotherapy but he told me that was Dr. Johnson's responsibility and he might have a different opinion than Dr. Williams. I wonder if they're debating whether to even do chemo! Wouldn't that be nice!

I'm hearing from a lot of people that they have friends who didn't lose their hair with chemo. So maybe I'll be lucky.

Tonight Dave and I are going to paint together. Tomorrow I'm not going to go to work even though I have no good reason and we'll spend the day at the house together. That will be nice.

Wednesday, December 18, 1985

Pregnancy 25 weeks, 4 days

A.D. 1 week, 6 days

1:00 p.m.

After talking to the radiologist yesterday, I'm convinced that it's better for the baby to be inside while the radiation therapy is going on. I kept asking what the danger was and all they really know is that there is an increased incidence of childhood cancers among children that have been radiated. That includes children radiated outside the womb. But not every child exposed to radiation gets cancer. A baby at 28 weeks has to go through daily chest X-rays anyway. Babies at 32 weeks are much less likely to have such severe problems, especially if the drug can be given to speed up the maturation of the lungs. So our minds are made up – take the baby at the last possible moment before chemo starts – if it starts. Maybe we'll be lucky and get out of it altogether and we can have the baby when it's due! But I'm prepared for a C-section at the end of January at any rate.

Today we're painting at the house. I opened all the shutters and curtains and it's so bright and sunny in here! We're really happy with our house. It'll be a great place to come home to every day.

Tomorrow I have to be at the hospital at 6:00 a.m. Choke, gag! I can't even get up then, much less already be somewhere! I hope I make it. The surgery is set for 10:00 a.m. I'm preparing for uselessness by painting and unpacking at the new house – I'd like to feel like I did something. My arm feels better all the time (that won't last long). The only thing that bothers me is stretching it to paint ceilings and such. I'm so used to being self-sufficient. I hope I won't be out of commission for too long.

Mom's going to spend the day with me at the hospital. She rearranged her schedule. I'm so glad she's back! I told all my friends to come visit when I thought I'd be in for a few days. Now it looks like they're all coming on Thursday – we're going to have a party!

Thursday, December 19, 1985

Pregnancy 25 weeks, 5 days

A.D. 2 weeks

5:20 a.m.

Well, today's the big day. I'm so nervous I have gas ("nerve gas", I call it). I'm extremely thirsty, too, but I'm not allowed to have anything to eat or drink. I thought I wouldn't be able to get up – I was awake since 3:30 a.m. I hope everything goes well. Stay in there, baby!

9:00 a.m.

Dave just left to get the move rolling. We stayed at Mom and Dad's house last night. I was exhausted and went to bed at 9:00 p.m.

The surgery went well. Dr. Williams said he found the cavity where the lump had been and just cut around all inside it. Then he sliced up what he took out to look for clumps of cells but couldn't see any. He also took out the little lump on my left rib cage and said he was sure it was just a fatty cyst. There must be something my subconscious knows that I'm not aware of, because when I was thinking, "if I had any more lumps, they would be ... here," my hand went straight for the place where that little lump resided. Strange, but true. It was like a Ouija board.

My perception of the surgery was not as easy as Dr. Williams'. I felt uneasy going into it, it took 1-1/2 hours, and I got terribly sick when I came out of it. I threw up five times, and I hadn't eaten since 9:30 p.m. the night before! It was terrible. And then the rest of the day people kept calling and visiting and I was just so out of it — all I wanted to do was sleep. Christopher, the anesthetist (not the same as anesthesiologist, he informed me), told me right before we left that they had given me some narcotic to regulate my blood pressure, so that was probably what made me throw up (narcotics always make me sick). I wonder if something did go just a little bit wrong during the surgery, to make me so apprehensive about it? Anyway, I'm not looking forward to going in for more surgery in five weeks.

Hopefully a spinal won't leave me feeling so terrible.

Dr. Williams came by to say the surgery went well, and told us that the chest X-ray was clear. Dad went out in the hall for a while and when he came back his cheeks were wet and his eyes were red. Dr. Williams said that he expected the scan to look good, since chest X-rays used to be the only thing they had to find lung tumors and CT scans hadn't been much of an improvement on them.

Yesterday I had a sonogram but they didn't tell me any results. They gave me a picture but it doesn't look like much. It was very interesting while it was going on, though, because it was easy to tell what was being shown as the technician moved the detector around. At one point she showed me a little arm (everything looked so little) and I felt and watched the baby move that arm!

After the sonogram, Dave came in and we went to the NICU. The babies were so small! But they all seemed well taken care of and somehow at peace. The place was bustling with activity and everyone seemed very caring. We talked to two doctors there who were very sympathetic. They showed us the babies from the tiniest intensive care patients to the ones that only needed to grow before going home. The babies at 31 weeks varied from needing a respirator to breathe for them to only needing a higher oxygen content than normal air. Their little arms were the size of my fingers and their little feet would fit inside a quarter. It's amazing that they make it.

We were very impressed with the NICU and we think our baby will receive excellent care there. We'll be able to visit or call at any time and they even have a "nesting room" where parents can sleep with their new baby and take care of it when it's almost ready to go home, but still have a nurse close by in case they panic.

I feel trapped by my own body right now. I wish I could get out and get away from all this tension. I still worry about working, taking chemotherapy and trying to go visit a teeny baby all at the same time. And even worse, taking care of such a little one at home with all the rest. At least we have family nearby. I think I'll be forced to go to six-hour days until sometime after the baby is home. Maybe when it sleeps through the night. I'll want to take time off when the baby first comes home. Oh, well, take it one day at a time.

Right now I feel terrible. My throat is sore from the tubes and all the muscles in my upper body are sore. From throwing up? Or from sweating all night in that hot hospital room? I don't know if I'm going to be able to direct traffic at the new house. We're going to be moved in today!

Oh, yes, I asked the doctor at the NICU about breastfeeding and she thought the mother's breast milk was great but they wouldn't feed a preemie anyone else's milk because the baby's immune system is immature and someone else's milk could have some things in it that the baby couldn't handle. But formula fed babies grow just as well. She also said that breastfeeding or pumping can be very draining, especially if I'm undergoing treatments myself, and it would be better to save my energy for visiting the baby as often as possible. The expected homecoming date for a preemie is the original due date, although some come home earlier and some later. I hope ours is a real trooper. She said that at 31 weeks very few babies die, so that's a comfort.

Monday, December 23, 1985

Pregnancy 26 weeks, 2 days

A.D. 2 weeks, 4 days

8:30 p.m.

We went Christmas shopping today for the first time this year. It was hell. Christmas should be fun but for me it's just the straw that breaks my back. But I couldn't stand not having anything to give anyone, especially since they're being so generous to us. I can't believe Christmas will be over in three days and I won't even have had a chance to welcome it, much less get ready for it to be over. I always get a little depressed when Christmas is over. We still have a lot to do at both houses – clean out the old one, set up the new one and fix the electrical wiring in the new one. Dave discovered that most of the house isn't grounded although they made it look like it by putting three-pronged receptacles in. So poor Dave has to fix that before he can hook up the appliances and we can live a "normal" life again.

Yesterday my old college roommate Maria came over and helped unpack. The kitchen, living room, bedroom and TV room look like they're in order, while the library still looks like a hurricane hit. We still have to get our pictures from the old house. I want to get the bedroom all snuggly and work my way out from there. There are so many things to do! At least we're to the point now where we can wake up, take a shower and eat a cold breakfast without major preparations. That's one step better than this morning!

I get depressed and overwhelmed when I think about what's coming in the next few months. Everyone's being nice and supportive now, but they can only keep that up for so long before they'll want my problems to go away. And I'm going to need help all the time for at least four more months. God, it's not fair to be stuck like this!

Wednesday, December 25, 1985

Pregnancy 26 weeks, 4 days

A.D. 2 weeks, 6 days

Christmas morning

8:45 a.m.

Christmas has dawned white and sunny. I'm feeling a little bit in the Christmas spirit now – we got everyone presents and wrapped them and they're all in the living room so it looks Christmassy in there. We never did manage to get a tree but the people I worked with in Indiana last summer sent a bouquet made up of white carnations, pine cones and pine branches. It's very pretty and I arranged the presents around that.

My arm looks like an elephant stomped on it – the entire upper arm is yellow, red, purple and black. But my arm is fairly useful – the only things I can't do are ... well, there are a lot of things I can't do yet, but I can do most everyday things without help. The scar looks pretty mean – it's about five inches from the top to the bottom of my arm and it has 17 stitches in it. On my side it looks like he made 2 cuts, one about 1/2 Inch and the other about one inch. Those are just taped up. I promise not to wince when he pulls them off. Maybe I'll pull them off myself.

Dave and I have been struggling to be in the Christmas spirit. Usually we manage for a few hours and then say, "What's the use – this is the worst Christmas we've ever had!" Then we try to count our blessings and decide it could be worse – but not much.

Right now we're getting ready to go to Mom and Dad's house for Christmas breakfast. I'm really looking forward to it. Then we're going to see Dave's parents and grandparents for dinner. I think it's going to be a nice day. I'm not going to be bummed out at all today. Merry Christmas!

10:00 p.m.

Christmas was nice. We made out like bandits because everyone feels sorry for us. We got several really big gifts. But the best part was just relaxing and being together with family.

Yesterday we took it easy and tried to get the house a little more orderly. We got the stove hooked up – now we need to get food to cook on it. I chased around after my paycheck too – it seems it's locked up and I can't get it until 1986. I guess we'll be broke until Wednesday. Yesterday Marty and Laura came over and entertained us with their gossip. It was nice to have people in our new house.

Today we went to see Dr. Williams to get my stitches out and then Dr. Germaine to simulate my radiation treatments. I now have little dots tattooed on my arm to show the boundaries of my treatments. We start Monday at 3:00 p.m. I'm going to have to start going to work at 6:00 a.m. to get to Oakland by 3:00 p.m. But it'll be worth it, I guess, not to break up the day.

Dr. Williams told me they found a small clump of cancerous cells in the tissue they removed, but it wasn't visible to the eye. The radiation will take care of any more that size. He still thinks chemo is necessary. I'm getting anxious about that. I'd like to see Dr. Johnson, the oncologist, to find out how he feels and what it will be like. I still get the feeling that they disagree on my treatment, although it's just intuition, not based on any facts. At any rate, if I have to go through it, I'd like to be prepared and to also get ready for the C-section. On Monday I'll try to arrange an appointment.

I'm incredibly tired all the time. I'm into the third trimester now and beginning to feel very pregnant. I can't breathe lying flat on my back. Everything else on top of the pregnancy just makes me eternally pooped out. If only someone could give me some energy...

Sunday, December 29, 1985

Pregnancy 27 weeks, 1 day

A.D. 3 weeks, 3 days

1:30 p.m.

Today I am soooooo tired! We went to bed at around 12:00 last night and I woke up at 6:30 a.m. to go to the bathroom. After I got back in bed, the baby started playing inside me and I couldn't get back to sleep. I stayed in bed until after 10:00 a.m., but I never really slept anymore. I feel totally, completely drained of all my energy.

Yesterday we spent the entire day at the old house cleaning it up. It's all clean except for the basement, and that's Dave's territory. I had all kinds of plans for today but I just can't seem to get moving.

All the leaves on my favorite plant, my big ficus tree, are falling off. It doesn't seem to want to live anymore. I put it in the sun and I hope it comes back. I have a sentimental attachment to it, of sorts. I bought it on April 25, 1984. I had just put it in the shower to wash the dust off the leaves when my best friend Sue, who was my roommate at the time, told me she was feeling so bad that she wanted to go to the hospital. She ended up being operated on that night – an ovarian cyst had ruptured and she had three liters of blood in her abdomen. I came home at about 4:00 a.m. to find the plant still sitting in the tub. Later they thought Sue had a rare form of cancer so they operated again, but decided it wasn't cancer after examining her excised ovary and fallopian tube. That was the same time that Jeff's brain tumor was finally discovered, after a year of headaches. Two months later Sue's mother got hit by a pickup truck while crossing the street and never regained consciousness. Then in October one of my family's good friends got killed in a car accident of which we'll never know the cause. We had the feeling that by now we had paid our dues. By now I'm afraid to ever feel secure again. Couldn't we just go through a few years uneventfully?

I'm getting more anxious about the chemo. Yesterday I cried because I was so depressed that I wouldn't be able to breastfeed. But I'm not even sure about that until I've seen the oncologist. I guess tomorrow when I see Dr. Macintyre I can get more information.

I keep getting stuff in the mail about Lamaze class – it's starting on January 3rd, this Friday. I don't know whether to go or not? Tomorrow...

Monday, December 30, 1985

Pregnancy 27 weeks, 2 days

A.D. 3 weeks, 4 days

10:00 p.m.

Much as we appreciate people caring about us, we're starting to get tired of unsolicited advice. The other day Marty and Laura mentioned that Marty's mother had had cancer and become active in some cancer group where she came in contact with a woman who was also pregnant and had some form of cancer. This woman decided to delay treatment until the baby was born and everything turned out fine. Well, I can see how they meant it to be heartwarming for us, but in actuality it made us feel like jerks because we refused to risk my life for the baby. I had a hard time not saying something like "boy, was that a stupid decision!" Maybe in her case it was a good decision; we can't judge that. But we don't want our decision judged either – we spent a lot of time agonizing over it and a story like this just seems to diminish that somehow.

Then there are people in the medical field who either give a piece of advice or say "I've seen many cases like this turn out fine." It just irritates me because they don't know enough about my case to make any comparisons – it always makes me want to say, "Yes, but my case is unique." Even though I know they're just trying to be helpful, I wish they'd just keep their mouths shut. I have doctors. I'll go to <u>them</u> for treatment! (Whew, that feels better.)

I much prefer the interested, caring reaction of, "Oh, you have a lot to deal with at once; is there a way I can help?" That way I can ask for advice if I want it, or decline help if I don't want any at the time.

I guess what really annoys me is blind optimism: Knowing one person with cancer who made it and assuming my case is similar (I guess I'm talking about non-medical people now). I can't expect everyone to know about all the different forms cancer can take – after all, I didn't before I got it – but somehow it's still annoying.

Anyway, today I talked to Dr. Macintyre. She helped set up an appointment with an oncologist (Dr. Stevens, who is Dr. Johnson's associate) for Thursday. I told her I was anxious about the chemotherapy and she said that she thought Dr. Johnson was going to be against it, and since he's the guy to do the therapy, his opinion would have to have more weight than Dr. Williams' opinion. Although, she said, if I wasn't comfortable with Dr. Johnson's decision, she would get me another specialist to talk to. Then she asked if the C-section was set for four weeks from now and I said that I wanted to go to term if we weren't going to do chemotherapy. She replied that they would still want to do the CT scan on me as soon as possible, so going to term is probably out of the question. Not that I like it, but at least that settles that question. I could really do without chemotherapy – I almost feel elated when I think about not having it – but then I would always wonder if a few cells hadn't made it out to burrow in some other unsuspecting part of my body to ruin my life again a few years from now. Which is worse? Agony now, or risk of more later? Or is there a risk? I guess I find out on Thursday.

I called the Lamaze teacher to tell her I wouldn't be in class. She was the type of person that was easy to talk to (she had the right attitude). She simply listened and was interested and brought up two points I hadn't considered. One was trying to take a special class on C-sections; she said that Magee offered those. The other was to tell the doctors about my anxiety over doing chemo, working and having a preemie baby all at once. I've even written it all down, but I hadn't thought of mentioning it to the doctors. So those are two things I'll keep in mind. It's funny from what corners help will arrive – a voice on the telephone, a cleaning lady, a check-out girl at the grocery store.

It almost seems as it strangers are easier to talk to – maybe because you know you're not causing them any pain by being in pain yourself.

Dr. Macintyre was supposed to call back tonight but Mom invited us over for dinner, and naturally we couldn't decline, so Dr. Macintyre probably called when we were out. I was hoping to hear about the sonogram tonight.

Today I had my first radiation treatment. It was agonizing because they made me keep my arm in an unnatural position for over 30 minutes. They taped meters to my abdomen but only put a lead plate between my body and my arm. It seemed like I was awfully exposed that way. Tomorrow I'll have to ask what the meters said. The treatment itself was painless. The machine was a little scary – it was very big and ominous looking. The worst part was when they moved it and it swung in a big arc around me to rest underneath me. From that angle I really wondered if the baby was shielded. But what was scary was that the machine seemed so big but moved so smoothly – it seemed like it ought to fall over and make a big hole in the floor instead of moving so effortlessly.

So far I don't feel any side effects. My arm felt sunburned when I left, but that's all. My arm has been sore all day. I wonder if something is wrong or if it's due to my driving and doing more with it. I hope that's it. If it doesn't feel better tomorrow, I think I'll call Dr. Williams.

Nicolette's best friend Lisa's mother died of leukemia last summer. Lisa spent the night at Mom and Dad's house the other night and they told her all about me. She said very honestly that she thought I was lucky because they had caught it early and could probably treat it successfully. Now I don't feel especially lucky, but Lisa is a very nice girl and would never hurt anyone's feelings, and I do think I see her point.

Jane, a very dear friend of my mother's from when she was an exchange student in Vermont for a year, called from Panama while I was at Mom and Dad's house (she is a nurse in oncology and her husband is an oncologist, both in the Navy and stationed in Panama currently). Yes – she said something of the sort that I was just complaining about. But she also said something about preemies (she had one herself): the steroids they give for developing the lungs of the baby occur naturally, especially in mothers under high stress, such as drug abusers. Since I'm obviously under stress, possibly my body is rushing the baby's development on its own. Wouldn't that be nice?

Today I spent a good hour removing all the dead leaves from my plant and cutting back its branches. I'm hoping that I gave it a chance to expend all its energy on renewing leaves instead of wasting it on dying leaves. It looks pitiful. It has probably 15 leaves left. I hope it works.

1:30 p.m.

My first day back at work and I haven't done a thing yet. I don't even remember what I was doing two weeks ago and I really don't care too much. It's difficult to get motivated – but if I can get into something then I'll have a distraction.

Bringing in the New Year was a little of a bummer. Mom and Dad usually have a big blowout but this year they only invited Paul and Ans Biloen and Lisa and us. We invited Marty and Laura but they couldn't come. Since the Biloens are splitting up and she's going back to Holland, they weren't exactly cheery either. So we made the best of it, but it wasn't like previous years. Next year should be better.

This morning we went to the oncologist, Dr. Stevens, since Dr. Johnson was on vacation. Dr. Stevens thinks we should do chemotherapy. He explained a lot of things to us. One thing that struck me was that it seems pretty hopeless if it gets to the lungs. Then the only thing you can do is use chemotherapy to shrink the tumors each time they grow – but you can never get rid of them. Also we asked for statistics and he told us that in patients treated like I will have been, 10% get a recurrence in the same spot and 35-40% get metastasis (a migration of the cancer cells) to another location, mainly the lungs. So the odds aren't quite as good as I had hoped. He said there was controversy over using chemotherapy as a preventive measure[3], which it will be in my case unless they find something with the scans, but he felt it was worth it considering the alternatives.

He gave me a booklet in which he marked the drugs I would be getting – I'd get them once every four weeks intravenously and the possible side effects are: Nausea, vomiting, hair loss, lowered blood counts, blood in the urine, loss of appetite, and mouth sores. Sounds like a barrel of laughs. I'm just going to have to see how I take all this. At least I'm getting some time to get used to the idea. Obviously the baby will be taken at 31-32 weeks, but I feel much safer with that than 27-28. Grow, baby, grow.

I guess I should try to figure out what kind of work I was doing.

---

[3] "adjuvant chemotherapy"

10:30 p.m.

Ever since I heard that statistic, I've been feeling very negative. Being on the wrong side of 99.9% can ruin your confidence in being on the right side of 55%. I don't want to die. I don't want to leave Dave all alone. I don't know if I would miss him, but I have a feeling I would. It seems so lonely. And I know he would be lonely without me. Imagining us apart really breaks me up – we've only been together for such a short time, it's not fair that we should even have to consider these kinds of thoughts. We make plans for our house together and then reality hits – who knows if we'll even be able to afford the house through all of this?

We had a discussion about finances tonight. It all started when I brought home a paper on life insurance being offered by my company – they have to accept an application for up to $30,000 from any employee within 30 days. I had to laugh (grimly). Who would voluntarily insure <u>my</u> life right now? But part of it was also that they would insure Dave at group rates and I think that's worth it. So I applied for $30,000 for me and $100,000 for Dave – enough to pay off the house and pay for child care. The company already provides twice my salary, so adding $30,000 brings me close to $100,000, too. Anyway, we were discussing how much each of us would need without the other so matter-of-factly, while all the time in the backs of our minds we knew this was a more real possibility than it is for most young couples.

The financial discussion came later when I looked up the tax tables for last year and found out that I paid $1,200.00 less than the table says for a married couple and we haven't even paid any taxes on Dave's income. So I panicked and was asking if I should get my money out of the 401(k) plan in case we needed a lot of money for taxes. I had been counting on working full-time until April at least, getting my car paid off, and having extra money for taxes. But now I'm going to be off work two months earlier and I'll probably need more time off than I have saved up (although Terri was nice enough not to dock me the hours I took before Christmas). Plus, I'll have the chemotherapy to deal with. So I was expressing all this to Dave and he said that since I have to work for the benefits anyway" and my income is steadier and higher than his, he could work less or not at all and do the primary care-taking of the baby. Also he would try hard to sell the property in Butler to get some money in the bank to fall back on. This is the location of the cabin his family used to spend many summer weekends in, although the cabin itself has been knocked down. His parents recently told him he could have it, either to keep or to sell and keep the money. So now I feel a lot better – I would never ask him to give up his work, but I do think it's the best solution for now. So if I can also work a couple of days a week at home so I can rest when I need to, maybe it can be done. Maybe we'll do all right.

My ficus plant has all kinds of shoots coming out. My therapy is working! I was thinking of this plant as a symbol, and it's encouraging that my symbol is coming back from near-death. I'm going to be just like my plant.

Cookie (our beautiful long-haired fluffy calico kitty) has a funny bump on her nose. I wonder if she has kitty cancer? I'll give it one more week and then I'm taking her to the vet. That's all we need – our favorite kitty with health problems, too.

Mom came over to hypnotize me today, but my friend Carole was here and I didn't want to ask her to leave.

Mom says we should do it at her office with no interruptions. I'm getting to the point where I really need it – to do something for myself.

Tuesday, January 7, 1986

Pregnancy 28 weeks, 3 days

A.D. 4 weeks, 5 days

7:40 p.m.

Mom hypnotized me on Sunday and I feel much better. Being in a trance is strange because you're aware of everything around you and yet you feel like a block of lead and couldn't possibly move if you had to. But that lead feeling means you're deeply relaxed and you feel that, once you come out of the trance. When she suggested that my cells should search for the cancer cells and suck the life out of them, I could only find one. That made me feel a lot better about the possibility of it being in my lungs – a sort of inner peace.

I've been having a lot of strange dreams lately. In one I was helping a woman in labor find a place to give birth and she decided on a place right below a dam. I told her that wasn't safe because they might open the floodgates but she wouldn't listen. So I started walking to the edge, but before I got there they opened the floodgates and everyone drowned and I was carried over a waterfall into a raging river – but I was holding my breath and telling myself, "Just hold your breath and keep calm, you'll get to calmer water in a little while." That same night I dreamt that Carole went to the hospital to give birth prematurely and I thought she died. Then I was told she didn't die but I couldn't find her in the hospital. Then when I came home there was a card in the mail that had funeral information for both her and her baby and I cried from the bottom of my heart – the kind of crying that makes your lungs hurt.

Radiation yesterday took a long time because of all the shielding contraptions. Today took less time – they're getting used to the setup.

Everybody seems to have an opinion on how I ought to be treated – either the doctors are doing it wrong or they're not doing enough or they're doing it too early or too late. But who hears about it? I do! I've been put in the position of defending my doctors more often than I care to mention. I wish people who don't like the way I'm being treated would just go and tell the doctors themselves if they know so much! It's really getting on my nerves. Don't they realize that every comment about my treatment causes me worry and anguish that I've already been through once? I'd rather they leave me alone than they make me feel this way.

Dr. Williams said today that I have thrombosis in one vein and that's what's causing the pain in my arm. Instead of the blood finding another route when he tied off the vein, it backed up and clotted. But it will go away eventually. He seemed pleased when I said I'd seen Dr. Stevens and that he was going to do chemotherapy. When I told him what Dr. Stevens said about once it gets to the lungs, he said, "But it's not in your lungs!" I said, "How can you be sure?" And he replied, "I'd say you have one chance in a thousand of it having spread to your lungs." When I said I'd heard that statistic before, he said he knew a little more about it than my doctors did then. He said he wasn't worried about my arm. But he does want to see me again in two weeks. I think he's placating me.

9:15 p.m.

I saw lots of doctors today. First I saw Dr. Macintyre, who said she had just talked to Dr. Stevens. Dr. Stevens was trying to find out if the CT scan could be done while I'm still pregnant, the idea being that if I do have more in my lungs and I'm doomed anyway, we might change our thoughts on taking the baby early. As Dr. Macintyre was telling me this her eyes got redder and redder and finally the tears welled up. I was surprised – was she crying for me? She was: I think she was feeling sorry for me and putting herself in my place – after all, she's a few years older than I am, but she's also young, apparently healthy, and probably wants a family soon. I was really touched that she would care so much. But as far as the CT scan goes, I'd rather wait the next three and half weeks and then be able to undergo whatever I have to without the baby interfering. The baby will have a good chance at that age and I won't have to expend energy worrying about what my treatments are doing to the baby. She said if they don't find anything, they'll still want to take the baby early so I can have chemo – if they do find something, it'll be up to us to decide what we do. But I know if they would find something, we would still want to do something right away and we certainly wouldn't give up on me – we'd do everything possible to keep me alive as long as possible. The longer the better, since a cure could be found at any time. But first things first – I'd rather wait with the CT scan because I don't think I would be capable of continuing the pregnancy if I thought I was dying. So I'd rather be optimistic and believe that it hasn't spread to the lungs, and find out for sure when the baby is its own separate little being. Besides, Dr. Williams doesn't think it has spread, and he knows it from the inside out.

Then I saw Dr. Himes, who didn't want to set a date for the C-section right away, but he did say that the sonogram showed everything is normal. The baby's weight was judged at about 2.2 pounds (995 grams) on December 20 (at 26 weeks), so it should be a good size five weeks later. I think the baby's going to be fine.

At radiation they said that my abdomen was getting less than 1/5 rad (a measurement of radiation levels), so the baby's getting less than that. That adds up to about one X-ray per week, and the baby would be getting more than that if it were already born, so I'm pleased. I found out that I'm getting 200 rads per treatment. Dr. Germaine said I could have a few days off when I have the C-section – it's the amount of treatments that's important, not that they are daily. Sometimes they have to take people off treatment for a couple of days anyway, if their skin reacts badly. But the radiation won't cause any problems with the surgery.

I was reading the stuff I was supposed to take to Dr. Stevens's office with me and one of the things was a letter from Dr. Williams to Dr. Macintyre in which, among other things, he thanks her for sending "such a nice couple" to him for advice. I always thought he liked us.

Cancer is such a strange thing ... I feel perfectly healthy and yet I have a life-threatening illness. If I were to feel ill, I would probably already be past help. How disgusting! I'd like to feel comparable to how I am, so I can tell from the way I feel, not from diagnostic tests, how I really am.

I told Dr. Macintyre about the hypnosis and she said it was a good idea and we should keep it up. I guess we will, if we can ever find time between treatments.

I asked Dr. Himes about C-sections and he said I should be out in four days or so and can walk as soon as the spinal wears off. He wants to try the drug that develops the lungs (I can never remember the name – Beta ...?) although it is true what Jane said about mothers under stress – he said there's hardly ever a baby born to a heroin addict who has lung problems. Ironic, huh? So the C-section doesn't sound too bad and the baby will probably be all right.

We're going to be optimistic – the baby's going to be fine and so am I. I refuse to become critically ill – I just have too much to do.

Oh yes, Dr. Himes doesn't recommend returning to work less than four weeks after a C-section, so I don't know what to do. He said he'd write me an excuse for eight weeks and maybe Stevens would write me one for longer – if I want to go to long term disability. (That's the way he talks, "Stevens" instead of "Dr. Stevens". He's very casual; that's what I like about him.) Oh, well, one day at a time.

2:15 p.m.

I'm on a downhill slide. It's hard to take life normally when it's possible that you could be terminally ill. I feel that leaded, lethargic feeling again, as if all the energy is being drained right out of me. Yesterday I stayed home from work because I felt like I was on the edge of a cold – sore throat, stuffy nose, headache, etc., but also because I was so tired that I had circles under my eyes.

Wednesday night Dave was telling me how lonely he would be without me – how he wonders if he would ever smile again, or even feel like smiling, if I'm gone. I knew he felt that way (it's the same way I feel about him), but to hear him say it just made me feel so sad. I don't know what would be in store for me if I died, but he knows what would be in store for him. I think in a lot of ways it's harder on the person who's going to be left behind, because that person's life is suddenly so empty. And he doesn't get nearly the support that I get. He has to comfort me when I get scared, but there's no one there for him when he gets scared.

It takes a lot of energy to deal with the uncertainty of whether I even have a chance of being cured. I think about things that just drain me. I think about Dave alone with a baby, or about him meeting some girl in a few years and saying, "My wife died of cancer when she was 26, or my parents at my funeral. I remember how much we cried the week that Dee was in a coma before she died – how awful it was to know that someone we loved was dying, and I don't want the people I love to have to go through that for me.

On Wednesday I said we were going to be optimistic, but it's a little more difficult than I anticipated.

I wonder if all this is good for something? Say I have the scan and there's not a trace of anything in my lungs, and I go through the chemotherapy and my 30th birthday comes and goes, will all this worrying and wondering now have any value? Am I supposed to be preparing for the worst case to appreciate anything else I get?

Friday, January 17, 1986

Pregnancy 29 weeks, 6 days

A.D. 6 weeks, 1 day

10:30 p.m.

I've been on an even keel since Saturday. Writing down all the stuff that was weighing me down seemed to just lift it off my shoulders and make it possible to live normally again. In general, weekdays keep us too busy to worry too much. Weekends seem to be tougher.

Yesterday I hooked up a video display terminal from work and got it working at home, so now I'm all set to start doing some work from home. They've been really good to me about my hours there – everyone knows I haven't been putting in full eight-hour days, but they don't complain about it and I still write it down as eight-hour days on my time sheet. I do seem to have my mind in gear, finally. I'm getting some work done – just not up to my normal capacity.

Mom called the other day and said she's donating Nancy (her house cleaner) to us once every two weeks. That is wonderful!

My pregnancy took a turn for the worse this week – between Tuesday and today I've gained five pounds and they all seem to be in my feet and hands. My shoes and rings are all too tight and my feet hurt all the time. My back hurts a lot, too, and I can hardly breathe lying down. I have to sleep on three pillows and I still get up at least once at night. I'm kind of glad I don't have to go through this for another 2-1/2 to 3 months!

Everyone is bugging me about the date for the C-section. I wish I knew it myself, but it depends on when chemotherapy starts and apparently that decision isn't being made. I expect it will be the first week in February now (past 32 weeks!) since I've had a few treatments skipped due to holidays and maintenance, so the treatments will extend into the third week in February. Maybe I'll find out on Wednesday, when I go see Dr. Himes again. I hope I don't have toxemia. I'm going to quit eating salt and junk food.

Maria told me the other day about an anti-cancer diet that cured some friend of a friend of a friend. Hah! I can see how a good diet can't hurt, but a cure? I'd have to be desperate to believe that.

Saturday, January 18, 1986

Pregnancy 30 weeks

A.D. 6 weeks, 2 days

10:00 a.m.

I'm 30 weeks today! The baby won't be born for at least 1-1/2 more weeks, possibly 2-1/2, so now the baby will have a much better chance than before – and every day improves that chance.

I talked to a woman yesterday at radiation therapy. Her husband is terminally ill with cancer of the pancreas. She kept saying, "Well, you just take it one day at a time." That must be a common attitude among people dealing with cancer. She said she had the same problem with people "knowing someone with cancer who was cured" and also bringing up all kinds of weird cures (like the diet). She said it drives them crazy, too. To illustrate the "one day at a time" philosophy, she told me about a time they were driving on the highway (she and her husband and their two daughters) and the front tire blew out and they barely missed going under a semi. This was just after they were told nothing could be done for him. "So you see," she said, "when your time comes, your time comes and there's nothing you can do to stop it. But you have to be glad for every day you've got." Amen. Her husband looked pretty bad. What's really sad is that he went to doctors for eight months saying there was something wrong with him and they just kept telling him it was all in his head. Then, when they found it, it was too late. Just like what happened to Dolf (Dad's best friend). It makes you want to shake those doctors to knock some sense into them – when are they going to realize they have to <u>listen</u> to their patients?

She also had some good news for me. Fifteen years ago her son was born two months early and had hyaline membrane disease (although he weighed 5 pounds, 9 ounces). It was touch and go for a while, but now he plays every sport in high school and he's over six feet tall. So even if a baby has problems, there's hope yet.

Monday, January 20, 1986

Pregnancy 30 weeks, 2 days

A.D. 6 weeks, 4 days

7:30 a.m. (before work)

We had a great weekend! We spent the whole time puttering around the house doing small projects. The house is shaping up. We put in a new phone jack in the study and rearranged it so it was optimal for both of us to work in. Then I made shades for the windows. I found a perfect material for the room – hues of red and purple that looked Scandinavian and pulled together the red rug and the teak furniture.

Then last night we had Mom and Dad over for dinner, which was very relaxed and enjoyable (never got a new hypnosis tape, though). Mom dragged me upstairs to decide what to do about the baby's room. It just dawned on me that we only have one or two weekends left before I have an operation and we have a baby!

... And find out whether I have terminal cancer or not. I don't want to know. I'm not ready yet. Not to give up the baby from my body nor to find out about my cancer. I guess we'll just have to concentrate on getting ready for the baby and to not to think about the other thing – can't do anything about it anyway. And there is a lot to be done for the baby.

9:00 p.m.

Dr. Macintyre called today. She said Dr. Stevens was supposed to call me last week and that's why we hadn't heard from her last week, but he didn't call that I know of. She said he had told her he wanted to give me one to two weeks off after the radiation before starting chemotherapy. So we could have the baby at 33-34 weeks! I know two people who had babies at 33-34 weeks and took them home within 10 days. On the other hand, my scan will have to wait that much longer, too, so we'll be uncertain that much longer. Dr. Macintyre said that when I go to see Dr. Himes on Wednesday, they'll have some dates for me. I told her about the days I've been getting off from radiation for various reasons, and she seemed shocked. She said, "No one told me that!" She was wondering if Dr. Stevens knew that – she said she'd tell him before Wednesday. (I had two days off for maintenance of the machine, and today because it's Martin Luther King's birthday and the staff has the day off.) The ending date for radiation is already in the third week of February and maybe later. We could have a Valentine baby.

One of the older men at work came down to "cheer me up" today. My office mate, Max, told me he had said to her, "We have to keep her spirits up." She tried to tell him my spirits were fine because she knew he didn't do much for me, but I happened to be lucky enough to be in when he came down the second time. This is how the conversation went:

R – "Hi, how are you?"

M – "Fine, how are you?"

R – "Good. How do you feel?"

M – "... better all the time."

R – "Good – and how are you emotionally?"

M – "Okay ..."

R – "Good, because I was going to come down here and spank you if you were depressed!"

Spank me indeed! As if I don't have a right to get depressed about this if I want to! Luckily he got a phone call soon after that and had to leave my office. If anyone else wants to cheer me up like that, I might as well shoot myself! Dave said I should respond with a straight question: "Why should you want to spank me if I were depressed about this?" Good idea. I'll use it if the occasion presents itself again.

They took the money out of my paycheck for the life insurance, so I guess now we're both covered. Whew! What a relief!

Last night at dinner we spent a long time discussing the little duckies I wanted to paint on the walls in the baby's room. Mom kept drawing and redrawing the design, and, from the glint in her eye, I get the feeling I won't have to paint any duckies myself. Mom has an artistic urge that can't be matched. When she made her shades, she made entire farm scenes on them and took over a year to finish them. In contrast, I don't start something I can't finish in one weekend (and if I can't, I often abandon it – ask Dad about reupholstering his chair! I started and abandoned that seven years ago.) I'm starting to look forward to doing the baby's room – that's the first step to getting it done, I guess.

Tuesday, January 21, 1986

Pregnancy 30 weeks, 3 days

A.D. 6 weeks, 5 days

9:20 p.m.

Today I saw Dr. Williams again. He's such a nice guy! I told him how no one was getting anywhere on the date for the chemotherapy and the C-section, and he said he would call everyone and get it arranged. I know he will, too. He isn't worried about the vein that's hurting, but he doesn't like the swelling in my arm. If it's not down in another two weeks, he's going to "do something about it." He's such an interesting person – he's got immense power – he's an expert, he's the chief of surgery at a major hospital, he says things like, "we should validate parking tickets. I'm going to get that done." and you believe him. Then on the other hand, Chuck, a salesman at work who is good friends with him, says he gets depressed. And tonight, when I mentioned we were going to have chicken piccata, he said. "Who's making that?" and when I said, "Dave, of course," he started talking about food in the same enraptured way Dave does, so I knew he was something of a gourmet. And he plays tennis. I wonder if he's married? A nice person like that should have someone – except he does seem to be working all the time. Maybe when this is all over we can invite him over for dinner and we can get to know him more as a person. He did give me a little speech today about how he felt this was a good way to go about the treatment and if I should have a recurrence, he would look anyone in the eye and say that he had done the best that could be done for us (me and the baby). But what he was hoping for was that in five years we would have a healthy five-year-old with a healthy mom. Me, too!

I asked if they were going to come visit me when I was back in Magee-Women's Hospital and they (he and his nurse) said, "Every day." Then he added. "I'll be there for the C-section." I don't know if he meant it, but that would be nice.

At radiation therapy today I saw a little girl who was losing all her hair. She must be two or three. She had marks on the side of her head, so I guess she has a brain tumor. She was such a pretty little thing and I'm sure her blonde hair used to make her look like an angel. Now she looks so pitiful. Maybe I'll get to know her if her treatments coincide with mine. I'd say it wasn't fair for such a little one to have to go through this, but by now I know life ain't fair. But it must be horrendous for her mother to watch her baby suffering. I hope I won't have to go through something like that in the future.

Dave went to visit his grandparents today. He's worried that they're going to die soon. Grandpap is 81 and Grandma is 80 or so. Grandpap is in pain all the time. He told Dave that he's been dead for a while now – what kind of life it is when you walk from your bed in the dining room to the living room and that's it? It seems like the death of one of them would lead to the death of the other – they've been married 61 years and are still in love, so I imagine being without each other would be intolerable. I just hope (selfishly) that they keep going for just a year or two longer – it would be just too much for us now. We know they have to die sometime, but we'd miss them too much to bear, so we just have to hope for their strength. Besides, they have to know their great-grandchild.

Grandpap is going in the hospital tomorrow. He told Dave that if they make him stay, he won't come back alive and he doesn't want to die in a hospital. God, I hope they leave him alone tomorrow!

Wednesday, January 22, 1986

Pregnancy 30 weeks, 4 days

A.D. 6 weeks, 6 days

8:00 p.m.

Grandpap made it home from the hospital. I guess he'll be all right. I just started feeling like I'm getting the flu – stuffed up, headache, nauseated. Now I realize fully how terrible chemotherapy will be – six months of feeling sick! Yuk! I'm going to try to sleep it off in a few minutes.

I saw Dr. Himes today. He said that Dr. Macintyre said that Dr. Stevens said I'd get two weeks off between radiation and chemo. Nothing like hearing it from the horse's mouth. The "horse" is supposed to call me soon (yeah, like last week!) but until then I'll believe Dr. Macintyre. So the baby can be born after radiation.

I pumped Dr. Germaine for a finish date and he told me to count on more or less 22 more working days. That puts me at February 21st, one day shy of 35 weeks! The baby'll probably come home with me! I'm just going to tell Dr. Himes that's when it'll be and we'll all have to live with it from then on. No more horsing around! I'll be able to breastfeed for two weeks! I'm happy (sick, but happy)!

11:20 a.m.

Dr. Stevens finally called last night. He said that he would like to do a lung scan so that if we find cancer in the lungs, we can let the baby go to term – treatment wouldn't be curative then, only life-prolonging. He also said he would definitely give me two weeks off between radiation and chemotherapy. I asked if surgery could help if there were few and small enough nodules in the lungs and he said it would definitely improve the prognosis.

In that case, I don't want to know until we can go right ahead and do something about it without worrying about the baby. I couldn't go for eight to twelve weeks knowing and not being able to do something. Taking the baby at 35 weeks is a negligible risk – they call 36 weeks full term. And then if there's nothing, we can go right ahead with the chemotherapy and if there's something we can go ahead with surgery. (Not again! Yuk!) I always get depressed when I talk to him. I don't expect or intend to have any cancer in the lungs, so this is the best way to go about it.

I guess what upsets me is that we had a plan and now he's throwing more uncertainty into it. He makes it look like we might be taking unnecessary chances with the baby's life and I keep thinking about that and wondering if it's true. The radiologist he talked to at North Hills Passavant Hospital said that he could shield the baby enough to get a good lung scan. Then we would know one way or the other. But if I know I have it in my lungs, how can I stand not doing something right away? And if it isn't in there they want to take the baby at 35 weeks anyway. Would it be such a big risk to the baby to be born at 35 weeks that I should go untreated for 5-7 weeks longer? And why don't I want to have that scan? Is it because I'm afraid of what I'll find out? I think that's it. I really can't stand to deal with anything else until I'm by myself again. I guess four more weeks aren't going to make much difference to me and they're the important weeks to the baby. The baby will still be older than Barb's daughter Alexa was, and she didn't have any problems. After the baby, I can have all the tests in the world. I'm sticking – baby February 21st, tests afterwards.

Tuesday, January 28, 1986

Pregnancy 31 weeks, 3 days

A.D. 7 weeks, 5 days

5:10 p.m.

The space shuttle Challenger blew up this morning. What a tragedy! I feel so bad for the families of the crew members, but especially the family of Christa McAuliffe, the teacher on board. It was supposed to be such a triumph, the first civilian in space.

On the news they just said that the crew collectively had 11 children. How terribly sad!

On one report they said that the teacher must have been aware of the dangers to her life – she took out a million-dollar insurance policy on the mission.

President Reagan put off the State of the Union address because of this. He made a sad speech on TV at 5:00 p.m. today.

He addressed some of it to the school children who were all watching today to see the lessons the teacher was going to broadcast from space. He assured them that the space program will continue and there will be more civilians going up in the future.

When I was a kid I told Dad I wanted to be an astronaut. He said I should be more realistic and become a doctor. But I always had it in the back of my mind.

Thursday, January 30, 1986

Pregnancy 31 weeks, 5 days

A.D. 8 weeks

8:30 a.m.

I'm at work, but I'm so bummed out I can hardly work. It all started on Friday, when Dr. Stevens called. He could have put it a different way – he could have just said we could do the CT scan to ease all our minds. The way he said it made it sound like he thinks it is in my lungs. Well, I'll see him Tuesday, so I guess I can ask him about that then.

Then on Sunday, Mom came over to hypnotize me. That didn't go as well as the first time but now we have a good tape – except who has the time to use it. After we were done, she called Dad to come over because he had said that he wanted to, only by the time we were finished, he really didn't want to anymore because he was busy doing other things. The reason for him coming over was that they had bought the chest of drawers for the baby that I had told Mom I liked. So it was a nice surprise. But before we could even get the dresser upstairs, we had another of those famous "incidents" between me and Dad, so the day was ruined – and we were still low from Friday anyway. What happened was this: We were eating the scones Dave made and Dad was putting preserves on his. I was waiting for him to give the preserves to me but he just kept pouring it on, so I said, "Hey, Dad, you would have yelled at us for putting that much on when we were kids." I was just trying to hurry him up, but he freaked out – he took the preserves on his scone and threw them on my plate – they spattered all over. After a shocked silence, we tried to behave normally again, but everyone was embarrassed and he was obviously angry. He left shortly after that. You wouldn't think that such a little thing would be a big deal, but it goes back to his childhood and it's also the relationship between the two of us. His mother used to beat him a lot – she'd fly into rages over the stupidest things. Also, he was a child during the war in occupied Holland, and he was always hungry, especially during the "hunger winter" between 1944-1945, when in Amsterdam there was no food because the Germans intentionally kept it out, and 50,000 people starved to death. Dad was in Amsterdam that winter. He was probably yelled at a lot for pigging out – putting too much jam on his bread, for instance. Well, all through my childhood he yelled at us for the same thing – he ruined many meals for all of us. And all the while he would be doing just what we were being punished for. I never thought much about it, though – I just assumed that was the way fathers behaved and tried not to do the things that made him mad. What I said to him was just a statement of fact and not any judgement, but I guess it triggered such a strong emotional reaction that he couldn't control himself. There's also the significant fact that I look a lot like his mother and act a lot like her (since he looks and acts like her and I'm his daughter).

But after all the incidents I've had with him, I know that if I try to talk to him about it, it will just become an issue of pinning the blame. He cannot see that his behavior was an over-reaction – he'll work it around so that I was a fire-breathing monster who should have been struck through the heart for what I did. And I don't want to put up with that, so I haven't talked to him at all since. I've talked to Mom, who relayed some of the things he's said. They were exactly what I expected: "Well, I've made an effort to stop yelling at them for that, so why should they torture me with it now!" and, "There's always a biting quality to that kind of comment." Of course he quit yelling at us! We're adults now! As far as the bite in the comment, maybe, but then he could have just said, "Excuuuuse me," like Steve Martin and left it at that. After all, who really cares how much jam he eats, for God's sake!

Anyway, it seems like a small thing, but it brings out some of the emotions we've never dealt with head-on and therefore it has escalated into a major problem.

Then on Tuesday the space shuttle exploded and that has the entire country depressed. I think I see why this hits so much harder than an airplane crash or a terrorist attack – it's the dreams of the future that were going up in that shuttle, and they were shattered with it. The entire nation was behind those astronauts, and now the entire nation mourns. Except for the idiots that called up TV stations complaining that their soap operas were preempted by coverage of the disaster.

So things were already going badly when I went to see Dr. Himes yesterday. On top of everything, it has snowed all week and traffic has been murderous, including on the way to Dr. Himes's. So when I got there, my blood pressure was 160/90 and after lying on my left side for 10 minutes it was 154/94. So now I have high blood pressure, which complicates a pregnancy. So Dr. Himes ordered a non-stress test and another sonogram for me and I can have a few more things to worry about. I have doctor's appointments coming out of my ears and I'm getting sick of it. Yesterday I went home after radiation and sat around for about an hour and a half and then worked from home till 9:30. Then I went to bed. Pregnant women are supposed to take it easy, and I don't have a minute's spare time. I don't think I can take this pressure much longer. I see now how smoothly your life has to run for you to be able to deal with this kind of thing. A few depressing incidents or statements can leave you wallowing in self-pity, while all the extra time required out of your day for treatments can leave you too tired to resist depression.

Dr. Himes tentatively set the baby's birth date for February 24th, since he operates on Mondays. I could go in on the 21st, but then I'd have Dr. Manson do the surgery and I don't like him. So I guess if I can hold on to my health and keep the baby in good condition, that's when it's going to be. I suppose I should call Mom and tell her. I just don't want to be confronted with more of Dad. Damn him! I need them right now! But I refuse to get dragged into another of those deteriorating "discussions" with him.

On top of everything, my arm is starting to get sore from the treatments, especially the underarm. I guess I'm not getting any breaks.

Wednesday, February 5, 1986

Pregnancy 32 weeks, 4 days

A.D. 8 weeks, 6 days

7:30 a.m.

Things are looking much better! We had dinner with Mom and Dad Monday and we got along fine (though we didn't talk about "the incident"). Yesterday I had my appointments with Dr. Stevens and Dr. Williams and a sonogram. The baby weighs 5-1/2 to 6 pounds already! What a bruiser! We're thrilled! Dr. Stevens said he had no problem with the way we want to handle it, so there's nothing to get depressed about. And Dr. Williams said again that he didn't think it was in my lungs and that he would call Dr. Stevens to discuss my case so that he is up to date on everything

Our baby will be able to come home when it's born. It'll probably weigh 6-1/2 or 7 pounds by then! How exciting! The baby looked good in all other ways, too.

9:30 p.m.

Writing makes me feel good, and I keep wanting to write, but there never seems to be any time. People keep telling me to take it easy, but it's impossible. This relentless pace – working, treatments, appointments, phone calls, life – is killing me. At least the baby will be born soon and I can take at least three weeks off.

Dr. Himes told me on Thursday that he wants to try inducing labor if an amniocentesis shows the lungs to be mature. At first I wasn't too keen on the idea – it means more tests and appointments for me and the uncertainty of labor which could end up in a C-section anyway (he said if I didn't give birth within 48 hours he'd do the section anyway). But the more I think about it, the better it makes me feel. No more surgery, no more drugs, and the experience of having a baby vaginally. Especially important is not being doped up when I first get to meet the baby. But also a quicker recovery would be extremely helpful.

9:50 p.m.

Boy, what a depressing day! First I found out that two people at work got promoted and I didn't. They both deserved it and I don't begrudge them their promotions, but I have been hoping for one for quite a while and it seems to keep passing me by. It's mostly bad luck at getting sick or pregnant at touchy times, plus projects on which I could have been a vital influence fell through. I got my performance review later in the afternoon and it was just the same as all the others – excellent work in most categories, close to it in all the others. But not good enough for a promotion. It's frustrating to work with a bunch of really bright people – you have to shine brighter all the time or you get lost in the crowd. And who has time to worry about that now, anyway? I guess I just have to keep plugging and be happy I have a job at all.

On top of that, Max (my office mate) went to visit her friend Vicki at Magee yesterday thinking she'd be up for having visitors after having a C-section on Saturday. But when Max got there, she found out Vicki had been moved to Presby and the baby was still at Magee. She went to see the baby and it looked so lonely. It was the only one in the nursery – all the others were with their mothers – and it was crying pitifully. Max said she wanted to take it home with her. She finally called Vicki at Presby today and found out that Vicki has leukemia! She's already going through chemotherapy. She'll be in the hospital four weeks and then go home. The baby is going home with her husband. You'd think the entire world had cancer! I feel so sorry for them. Leukemia has a much worse prognosis than a sarcoma and at least we have time to adjust to it before the baby arrives. And we won't have to be separated. I'm going with Max tomorrow to visit Vicki, since I'll be there anyway and it might help her to talk to someone who has an idea of what she's going through. I feel sorry for her husband. He probably doesn't know what hit him – and now he has to take care of a newborn baby, too. Poor guy. Plus, his wife might die – soon. I never thought I'd say this, but I feel lucky at this point.

Not to mention that Leslee's little boy is in the hospital, too. He got an ear infection so severe that he had to be operated on. And then he got the flu and was so sick that he vomited and wouldn't eat, which he's never done before. So now Leslee has to go to the hospital every day and she's almost 36 weeks pregnant.

To top the day off, when I went for my treatment today (25 out of 30!), the technician put tape right on the sore spot under my arm. It hurt so much that I started to cry and I got nauseated. It reminded me of waking up from surgery. After the treatment was over I felt weak and everyone was concerned because I was so white.

Two of the nurses sat and talked to me for a good half hour before I finally left. They are so nice! I have to be sure to bring them something before my last treatment – maybe a box of Valentine's chocolates. They suggested a couple of support groups we might want to contact – *I Can Cope* and *Take Each Day as it Comes*. But not right now. Maybe in a few months. We'll still be dealing with it by then.

I had an interesting dream the other night. I dreamt I went to the hospital to have the baby. I was in heavy labor when they put me on a cart to go to the delivery room. It was sterile and scary and there were two men I didn't know in there. My labor stopped. So they wheeled me back to the first room and there was a big healthy baby boy on the bed. So I started to play with him and finally I put him to my breast. That gave me a sexual type of pleasure and all of a sudden I felt something start to come out between my legs. I pushed and pushed and finally the whole thing came out. It was ugly! It was a black round thing with spider-like tendrils all over it. I especially remember two where the left arm should be and five where the right arm should be. Our kitty Cookie jumped on the bed and ate it. I was relieved that it was gone and went on feeding the baby.

I guess that the black thing could be seen as the cancer, and the dream means that taking care of the baby will help me eradicate the cancer from my body. Even if that's not what it meant, that's a useful way of looking at it!

An interesting note Vicki and I both spend a good part of our day in front of computer terminals. I wonder if that triggers some cancer gene in your body?

Pregnancy 33 weeks, 4 days

A.D. 9 weeks, 6 days

8:00 p.m.

I went with Max to visit Vicki today (I hadn't met her before, but I felt like we had something in common). She's a really nice person and seems to be in pretty good spirits. I brought along my booklet on chemotherapy and she seemed really pleased by that. She said no one had given her anything to read yet. But when she mentioned it to the nurse, the nurse found some other pamphlets for her. So I did some good. It was good for me to see someone in a position similar to my own and she seemed to appreciate it, too. She told me to come visit her when I was in the hospital and she could tell me about the first few days of chemo. I think I'll go see her on Friday and give her my phone number. I want to let her know she can call me when she wants to talk about what most people don't want to listen to, like dying or not being able to cope; the things I thought about a lot that she must also be thinking.

Her little baby was there. She was very pretty and petite – she weighed 6 pounds, 4 ounces and she looked like she'd fit in the preemie clothes Mom got. Ours will probably weigh about that much, too. Vicki looked very sad when the baby was taken away (as her husband,

Dan, and mother-in-law left). I don't know how I would handle it. I feel pretty lucky after all. Dan seemed to be taking it pretty well, but it's hard to tell.

I talked to Max about not getting promoted (she was one of the two who did) and just talking about it made me feel better. I think I'm ready to just keep plugging along until I'm all better and after that my past mistakes will have blown over and I can start working for it then. It's ironic that Max got the elusive project leadership role (that they say you need to be promoted) because I took the long-distance role in Chicago this summer, when I was thinking that going to Chicago would clinch my promotion for me. If I'd refused to go, the situation would have been reversed, and then what would be happening? But some good did come out of going to Chicago – I got pregnant (on a weekend home!) and we were able to buy a house from the extra money I was able to save by sharing an apartment with Terri (since the per diem payments were enough to live in a hotel). Max also brought up a good point – if they gave me a raise and then I got sick or went part-time, they wouldn't get their money's worth out of me. Oh well, I have more important things to worry about.

On Sunday, Mom and Dave's Mom are having a shower for me. I'm really excited – I can't wait to get all kinds of little baby things!

My treatments should be over by Tuesday, so I guess the baby will be born sometime next week. Fear and excitement intermingle.

4:30 p.m.

I just came back from a round of doctor's appointments. Today my blood pressure was good, my weight gain was minimal, and the non-stress test showed the baby was still in great shape. Dr. Himes also gave me an internal exam which showed my cervix is soft, I'm about 30% effaced, and my cervix will admit a fingertip (if it were tightly closed, it wouldn't admit anything).

Then I had a nice long talk with Dr. Paulone, the high-risk pregnancy doctor, who was a very reasonable person. Together we decided that we should skip the amniocentesis, since we wouldn't change our plans based on it anyway. Vaginal delivery is definitely preferred. It seems to do something to make the lungs mature if they're not mature. So now a C-section is a last resort. But now we have to wait and see what Dr. Stevens decides about the chemotherapy. If he doesn't want to give it, there's no reason to have the baby early at all. Except so I can have the lung scan. I guess I'll plan on going into labor Wednesday until I hear something different.

Pregnancy 34 weeks, 1 day

A.D. 10 weeks, 3 days

10:00 p.m.

Busy, busy weekend! Friday night we went out to dinner along with seven million other couples for Valentine's Day. Friday afternoon Dr. Himes called and told me to go to Magee on Wednesday around 5-6 p.m. and tell them I'm there to be induced. I'll get my prostaglandin suppository then (to soften my cervix). Thursday they'll start inducing. Friday they'll break my water bag and that should really get things going. Then my progress depends on me and nature and hopefully I won't end up with a C-section after all.

Dr. Williams called me back (I stopped by his office on Thursday to ask him about the chemotherapy). I told him what Dr. Stevens told me about the third opinion and considering not doing chemo if the third opinion was that it was low grade. Dr. Williams said he didn't think they would find that, since he had shown my slides to a number of excellent pathologists, but he would definitely talk to Dr. Stevens about his findings. I told him I would feel much better if I knew they had conferred with each other. He called me back a couple of hours later to tell me Dr. Stevens was sick but he would make sure to get in touch with him. He also wanted to know when the baby was going to be born and it sounded like he just wanted to know so he could make sure to stop by. He's such a nice guy!

I stopped to see Vicki again – the baby was there again, too. I can see that for her the distraction of the baby is keeping her sane. She said she didn't feel sick at all from the chemo. It's nice to have someone to talk to who also switches from chemo to formula in the same sentence. Apparently her chances of going into remission are good. I hope so.

So that was Friday. Then Saturday we had a little party here, which was nice, and today Mom and Dave's Mom had a shower for me at Mom's house. It was very nice and we got a lot of really neat things for the baby. All this is so exciting! Less than one week ...

Tomorrow is Dave's birthday and I haven't done a thing for it. I went to get him a tool that he's been looking at, but it's very expensive and I've been worrying about money lately. Of course, the tool could help him make more money. I'll have to decide pretty fast.

We've only been in the house two months and they've already nearly doubled our taxes. And the low taxes were part of the attraction of the house! Shit. There goes my raise – $50 a month, if I'm lucky enough to get that much. Oh well. I guess things will work out.

Pregnancy 34 weeks, 3 days

A.D. 10 weeks, 5 days

11:00 p.m.

Dr. Williams called today to say that he had talked to Dr. Stevens and his pathologists agreed with the ones Dr. Williams had talked to: "This is a higher grade lesion that should be treated with chemicals." I'm glad they all agree, but I can't say I'm elated. I didn't realize how much I was grasping at the straw of no chemotherapy until it was definitely taken away. Yuk.

Today was my last treatment. I brought in cookies and the nurses gave me a Teddy bear! Everyone was telling me to be sure to call when the baby is born. I was elated that it was my last treatment, but I will miss seeing some of those people every day.

I went to see Vicki again. She says she still doesn't feel sick – only tired. And her sister is a match for bone marrow, so they can try a transplant. If it works, she'll be cured. We talked about wigs together. It's still really sad to think about two new young mothers who have to go through chemotherapy to have a chance to stay alive. I hope things work out all right. She was crying when I came in and I was reminded of some of the early times when Dave and I felt that we ultimately had to face this by ourselves.

125

So tomorrow I go in to Magee-Women's Hospital. I finished making the lace skirt for the bassinet and Mom painted half of the duckies on the wall. They're adorable. Oma's antique crib isn't coming for another three weeks (Mom lent it to friends when none of us kids were even married yet). I'm disappointed – I really wanted to try the crib hammock with the beating heart in it.

I got Dave a small present and a cake and told him that as soon as we could afford it, we would buy him his tool. His birthday wasn't very special, and I feel bad about that. Maybe I can do something special for him sometime soon.

I'm nervous about giving birth. I hope it doesn't take too long. And I hope the baby's okay.

Monday, February 24, 1986

A.D. 11 weeks, 4 days

8:30 a.m.

Our baby died.

I went in on Wednesday night and they gave me a suppository which gave me cramps all night long. Then I was 60% effaced and 1 cm. dilated and they started a Pitocin drip which gave me irregular cramps. By the evening I was 70% effaced and 1 cm. dilated. The baby's heart beat was strong and regular. They decided to try more prostaglandin and gave me a sleeping pill. At 2:15 a.m. I was 2 cm. so the doctor on call broke my water and started the Pitocin again. The baby was still fine. I started getting contractions every 3 minutes for 60-70 seconds. I had to ask for drugs. By 11:30 a.m. I was 100% effaced and 4cm. dilated, but both the baby and I had incredibly high heart rates. They did some painful test to get blood out of the baby's scalp and that was inconclusive. So Dr. Manson decided to do a C-section. I was relieved. I had started to feel something was wrong about four hours earlier and was hoping they'd end it soon. During the C-section I was shivering uncontrollably. It was terrible. And then I heard the baby cry – "It's a girl!" – and it was all worth it. She weighed 5 pounds 13-1/2 ounces and she was beautiful. She looked just like her Daddy. I could hear her crying and then they showed her to me – her little face just peeked

127

out from between the blankets and the hat. She was beautiful. She had the most precious little mouth with a curved lower lip like a perpetual pout. They let Dave hold her and she started having trouble breathing so they took her to the NICU. I never saw her alive again after that. I never even saw her eyes. She hung on for eight and a half hours but she had some systemic infection that she just couldn't fight.

Every time Dave came back from the NICU he would give me worse news and then he would say, "She's so beautiful, she's so beautiful." He got to stroke her and see her entire body. At around 10.30 p.m. on Friday (she was born at 2:20 p.m.), Dr. Brown, her doctor, came to my room and said they had done everything they could and he didn't think she could make it. I said that I wanted to see her and he said he'd arrange it. But I had just gone through surgery and I couldn't go in a wheelchair. They finally called Dr. Manson to ask him what to do and he said to get me down on a stretcher. They put me on the stretcher, which was still agonizing, but when we got to the elevator Dr. Brown met us and said, "You might as well go back." I said, "She died," and started crying. It's so hard to cry when it hurts so much. I wanted to sob but I just couldn't tolerate it. He asked if we wanted to see her and we said yes. So he and a nurse brought her little body to us. The nurse broke down when she laid Gwynne down next to me. She was all purple from the low blood pressure but she was soft and warm and looked peaceful. She had dark hair and she was still beautiful. Those tiny fingers and toes. She felt so solid – I couldn't believe she was really dead. We didn't know that our entire family was still here in the hospital. Somehow they must have known, because they came up a few minutes after they took Gwynne away. We sent them down to the NICU to get their first and last look at her. The only one that didn't go was Dave's Dad. He stayed here and held my hand. He said he just couldn't go down and see her.

The last few days I've been so drugged that I haven't felt much of anything. Here's what Dave wrote the day after Gwynne died:

"Our baby has died. I, too, must write. Sorrow like I have never known envelops me. I did not know her, but she had become my world for a few short hours. When she was born I was to hold her for only seconds, seconds that now cause me pain. I can think of no other words to describe how I feel. Pain and hurt consume me and tie my stomach in knots. My love for my wife sustains me and reminds me of my responsibilities to her, myself and others. It also reminds me of the responsibilities I had to a precious baby girl. My baby is gone, but my care and love for her can never cease. One yet unanswered question torments me. Was I ever truly a "father"? True, I helped bring her into the world but I could do nothing to help her remain in it. I could do nothing as her tiny chest heaved for every breath. As I stroked her body I wondered if she knew it was the touch of her father. She gave no signs of recognition. She just continued with her life struggle. I had no chance to be a nurturer, nor could I assist her with the struggle. I was helpless. She was dying and I did not even know it."

The doctor just came in and told us the preliminary report said it was a Streptococcus B infection, which is devastating to babies. The bacteria reside in the vaginal tract of 10-15% of all women and it sometimes doesn't cause any trouble while at other times it causes the death of the baby – at any gestational age. So we don't have to blame ourselves for taking her early. It could have happened at 40 weeks, too.

Dave has made all the arrangements for the funeral. It's going to be Thursday at 3:00 p.m. and we're letting anyone come who wants to. Dr. Beattie, the minister who married us, is going to do a short graveside service and then we're going to return our little girl to the earth. Dave said it was incredibly difficult to buy a burial plot for your little baby. We'll dress her in some of the clothes that were already given to us and we'll put a nice soft teddy bear in with her. Someday we'll be with her again.

9:20 p.m.

Debbie, the nurse who took care of Gwynne the entire time she was fighting for her life, came up to see us just now. She baptized the baby when she started to look bad. We talked to her for quite a while – she took it badly herself. She told us that Gwynne had blue eyes. I wanted her to have seen someone in this world. Debbie said that Gwynne was a very special baby even in those eight hours that she took care of her. And Debbie told her that her parents loved her very much.

We told Debbie that we really appreciated the fact that she cared enough about Gwynne to cry when she brought her body up to us that night. It kind of gave us a feeling that she was cared for in all those hours that we were helpless. She told us that it was good to hear that we appreciated it, because sometimes she wondered why she would go through all that pain.

It's all so overwhelming that I can't keep it all straight. Dr. Brown came and talked to us for a long time. He also seemed convinced that this was something unpredictable that we couldn't have caused. The visits from Dr. Brown and Debbie gave us a certain peace of mind that we had been looking for since the 21st – just knowing that someone was constantly with her, looking out for her, trying to save her, and loving her. Debbie obviously loved her. She told us that we were special people and she felt confident that we would have another special and beautiful baby

I think right now the drugs and the physical pain are taking the edge off the emotional pain. It only seems to crop up periodically. I expect to feel a lot more grief once my body can stand it.

Tuesday, February 25, 1986

A.D. 11 weeks, 5 days

3:30 p.m.

It's so unfair! We tried so hard to do everything right! We took such good care of the baby. How could she be taken away from us? How could nature be so cruel as to take the dreams we had been nurturing and shatter them like that? She died from something totally unrelated to being premature or exposed to radiation. It would have happened anyway. But why us? I know it's the impossible question, but we accepted the fight with cancer without too much of a fuss – why do we have to be tested further?

Our beautiful little girl is dead. I don't think I can stand the pain. I only saw her alive once, I only heard her cry once and now she's gone. Dave was so proud and so in love with her, saying, "She's so beautiful," over and over again; he was so ready to nurture and protect her and instead he has to take care of me. Our little ray of sunshine is gone. If looking at pictures could make them wear out, the two we have of her in the NICU would be gone already. I just can't stop staring at that lovely little body and wishing that I could change her, rock her, feed that beautiful little mouth, take her home with me. I would gladly have suffered a severe illness if it could have kept her alive.

I know what Dave meant – it's so difficult to give up parenthood when you're not even sure you've experienced it yet.

I'll never forget my sweet adorable little Gwynne Elizabeth. I just hope her soul is somewhere beautiful and peaceful. I'm glad she didn't suffer long.

We're burying her in the Mount Royal Cemetery; a place I always thought looked peaceful as I went past. Dave bought a plot in a beautiful spot close to a tree where she can be buried and one of us will be buried there when we go. I hope that's not for another 50 years. Oma is flying over for the funeral. It will be nice to have her here. I'm putting the Teddy bear that the nurses at radiology gave me, in Gwynne's coffin with her. I've been sleeping with it every night and it's difficult to give it up – which is good because I want that bear to give her the softness, warmth and love that I've been pumping into it. She'll have a little friend as she slowly becomes part of the earth again. Mom is making a little quilt that has hearts on it for each member of Gwynne's family. That will go in her coffin, too. I hope that somehow she understood how much she was loved.

Wednesday, February 26, 1986

A.D. 11 weeks, 6 days

7:30 a.m.

Today should have been the happiest day of our lives, taking our baby home to live with us. Instead I wake up crying every morning and go to sleep crying every night even though it still hurts to cry.

Sometime in the middle of the afternoon I feel strong and start saying we're going to make it, but the rest of the time I'm just enveloped by the desire to have my baby. How can I go on? I wanted her for so long and I loved her so much. I can't stand to let her go.

A.D. 12 weeks

9:45 a.m.

Today we're going to bury our little girl. Yesterday Mom came over and we worked on the little quilt Gwynne's going to be wrapped in. I embroidered her name and birthdate on the satin square in the middle and Mom embroidered all the hearts of the family in a circle around her name: Mommy, Daddy, Oma, Opa, Uncle Hugo, Aunt Nicolette, Zwarte Oma, Witte Oma, Grandma, Grandad, Gram, Grandpap. Each person got a different heart which Mom appliqued on. Then Mom quilted concentric hearts starting in the middle of Gwynne's name. Everything is white except the names. That little girl would have gotten so much love if she had just lived. Why are there babies born with fetal alcohol syndrome and addictions to all kinds of drugs while our baby, who was so taken care of and loved, was born with an infection she couldn't fight? There was nothing wrong with her – she was perfect. But a killer was raging in her little body.

Every once in a while, I think I would just like to have a baby to take care of right now. But then I realize I only want Gwynne. Just Gwynne. I think Dave has his baby in me. I need a lot of care right now.

I got a very nice letter from Doris, our new secretary, saying how she feels for us because a long time ago she lost her little girl after eight years of waiting. She said that even though she knows it doesn't help to hear it now, time will heal. She also said that somehow we will have someone or something to compensate for the loss of our baby.

I have to concentrate now on getting through the chemotherapy healthy and fertile, so we can start on a new baby soon. It really scares me how that infection killed Gwynne – the key was that she had no more antibodies to fight the infection and that could happen to me during chemotherapy – I could be knocked out by almost any infection. So somehow I have to remain strong.

9:30 p.m.

It's over. The sun came out for us to put our little baby daughter to rest. Dr. Beattie gave a very nice service in which he mentioned many of the things that we have thought and talked about and then he said a few short words at the grave. There were a lot of people there – I didn't get to see who many of them were, and they left before I got a chance to talk to them. There was an outpouring of love from all of those people and there is comfort in that.

It feels peaceful to know where she is and that we can go visit her. The hill on which she's buried is visible from a road really close to our house — every time we go somewhere we can glance over at our baby.

Dave and I talked about trying to have another baby. A month ago, we were saying that we'd wait 3-5 years to make sure the cancer didn't come back, and that it would be irresponsible to have another baby if I might die. Now all of that seems useless. Why wait 5 years when I might die in a car accident? We both want to try again as soon as possible – maybe a year from now. With that in mind, it does seem possible to go on.

Friday, February 28, 1986

A.D. 12 weeks, 1 day

8:00 a.m.

My dear sweet little baby. Did you know how much I loved you? The moment I first heard you cry was the most precious moment in my life. And when I first saw your little face I thought I would die of happiness. Now I think I'm going to die of pain over losing you. You would have been a week old today – instead you're lying in a little coffin wrapped in all our love.

When they laid you in my arms after you died, you looked so peaceful. That's the only time I got to touch you, and you were so beautiful and soft. It is so hard to give you up. So hard.

I had imagined you in your bassinet next to our bed, waking up and crying and I would reach in and stroke you gently to let you know that Mommy was there. Then I would reach in to pick you up and I would put you between us and your Mommy and Daddy would just love you for a while in the morning. Now every morning I wake up and look at the empty space where your bassinet should be and my heart empties out all over again.

7:00 p.m.

Not only do I mourn my baby, I mourn my pregnancy. I mentioned earlier how I would miss feeling the baby moving around inside of me. Now I feel that loss doubly. Every day my body gets closer to its normal state – my stomach gets smaller, my breasts get lighter, I lose a little more weight – and each of those changes reminds me how permanent this is: I am no longer carrying my baby, my body is empty, and my baby has died so there is nothing to look forward to.

Dave and I were talking about how we had imagined her. He had thought of her little fingers grasped around one of his, of taking her for walks, of being there as she became conscious of the world. I had had conversations with her at different ages – at three about her, at six about kids teasing her at school, at twelve about boys. We had already woven her into the tapestry of our future. Now we have to pull apart the cloth and start all over again

We keep getting flowers – the house looks like a funeral parlor. I would prefer it if people would contribute that money to the American Cancer Society or the NICU at Magee, and I told some people that, but I guess that doesn't seem personal enough to them.

Today a package arrived in the mail. It was from Julie and I knew it had to have baby things in it – she asked me in her last letter what I wanted, and I had replied. I was helpless as I opened it – it was an adorable shirt with an elephant and a giraffe embroidered on it and a pair of bright red pants. It broke my heart all over again. In the letter along with it she asked if we would call and tell her when the baby was born. I couldn't face calling, so Sue offered to do it for me. I can't stand it when I call people and their initial reaction is, "Oh, hi, did you have the baby?" I just can't stand to tell them what I can still scarcely believe.

Saturday, March 1, 1986

A.D. 12 weeks, 2 days

8:00 p.m.

My right breast is hard and painful and is leaking buckets full. How much more do I have to take? Why does my body have to remind me that I have no baby to feed? I can't stand it; I can't stand it. It hurts so much. It's so unfair. I don't know if I have the strength left to go through chemotherapy now. Oh, God, I wish my baby were alive!

We bought a headstone for her today after we visited her grave. It was so small. Looking at headstones is so difficult. I don't know how Dave ever managed to arrange her burial plot and funeral. We had the man put "Our beloved daughter" above her full name, Gwynne Elizabeth Edwards, and her birthdate. But that doesn't convey all the feelings we have for her. Our precious little baby is gone forever and I'm so sad.

Sunday, March 2, 1986

A.D. 12 weeks, 3 days

11:00 a.m.

We've made it through another day. I hate it. I want time to stop – actually go backwards. I want to go back to the Wednesday I went into the hospital and get stuck there, forever pregnant but at least having the baby alive inside of me. I don't want to cope; I want to die. The only reason I want to stay alive is Dave – if I died he would have to go through this again, twice as hard, and I couldn't do that to him.

She would be nine days old today. I suppose soon I'll stop keeping track. It's not even the month she was born in anymore – time keeps relentlessly going forward when I want to stop it at the moment of her birth and somehow save her life.

People who have lost someone say it gets a little bit better every day. I don't want it to get better – I'm afraid to accept the death of my baby and go back to a "normal" life. I'm afraid to go through the chemotherapy – if she were alive I would go through it to be around for her but now that she's gone I'd have to go through it and risk never being able to have another baby. Not that another baby would ever replace Gwynne, but I want a baby so much and I have so much love to give. Right now the only baby I want is Gwynne, but I'm sure that if

142

I were to get pregnant again, we'd love that baby for itself.

9:30 a.m.

I still have so much trouble accepting that something so cruel has happened to us. Wasn't it enough that I had to have cancer? Why did our baby have to die, too? She was the only thing we wanted, why did she have to be taken away from us? I'll never be able to understand how this could happen. It just hurts so much.

My breasts are hard as bricks and after my shower they were leaking like faucets. There's nothing worse than a mother having breasts full of milk for a baby that's gone. It just makes me ache for her.

One of Dad's co-workers told him that he and his wife had lost their firstborn son when he was a week old and they still think about him and what he might be like today. They have a son my age, so this must have been over 25 years ago. I guess with the loss of a child you never get over it completely.

I'm getting more and more confused as to how it all happened. If this infection was already there, how come her heartbeat was so strong and healthy? Why were there only signs of infection after I'd been in labor for almost 48 hours? How could it have gotten to Gwynne and how could it have gotten strong enough to kill her?

And I'm so ambivalent about my own treatment now. I'm so tired, I need a break. I don't know if I can stand six months of worrying about what the drugs will do to me on top of the cancer, as well as grieving for my lost little one.

Today I get my lung scan. It just can't show anything. We just can't take any more of this. It just has to be clear.

10:40 p.m.

For the CT scan they asked if I was allergic to fish or seafood. I said no. Apparently I am. Thirty seconds after they started the I.V. drip of iodine "contrast" (fish & seafood contain a lot of iodine), I started sneezing, my nose clogged up and I got hives on my face. I was sure I was going to die on that table. They gave me a shot of Benadryl, which immediately cleared up my nose but also made me really woozy. The nurse went out to tell Dave to get the car and she started out by telling him I'd had an allergic reaction to the dye. Naturally, after the last few months, he assumed I'd either died or I'd been admitted in critical condition. By the time she got around to telling him they wanted him to drive the car up so I wouldn't have to walk, it was all a big relief to him. I'd better remember to tell people to assure Dave that I'm all right first.

I felt so lonely in the waiting area. One lady started talking to me and asked me why I was there. I told her a little about my cancer and she said, "You're young, you'll be all right." I started to cry. It seems like ages ago that I thought that, too. Here I am sitting with the front of my gown completely wet with milk stains for my lost baby, and someone tells me I'm going to be all right. I'm actually afraid to cross the street anymore because I don't consider it altogether impossible that I might get hit by a car.

Wednesday, March 5, 1986

A.D. 12 weeks, 6 days

8:00 a.m.

Early every morning my eyes fly open and I realize my baby is dead and I can't sleep anymore. We both miss her so much! We had envisioned her everywhere in the house. It's impossible to be in the house without thinking that she should be here. It's impossible to do almost anything without thinking that.

Yesterday we went to Sue and Rick's house to watch their VCR and on the way home I got upset because Rick had arranged to borrow a VCR camera that we could use to make movies of the baby so that we'd have them when we could afford a VCR. And that's what we should've been doing!

I want my baby so much! I need to have a little bundle to rock and cuddle and feed and take care of. I have so many images in my head that I just can't shake – of putting her in bed, getting her out of bed, feeding, bathing, changing her. I was so in love with her for as long as I knew I was pregnant, that I just can't stand for her to be gone. And yet I have to stand it. It just breaks my heart when I see in her pictures that she held her hand in the same position as in the last sonogram picture – the picture that we all called "Baby power" and took as a symbol that she was going to be all right. Even though

147

I scarcely dared to believe that I was going to have a real live baby of my own, I never dreamed I would have to go through the agony of losing her. How many times can I keep repeating how unfair it is? It's unfair, but it happened, and we have no choice but to accept it. But I keep thinking of all the things I would give up if I could just have my little Gwynne.

Today we go to Dr. Stevens to find out about my scan and my heart study and my chemotherapy. I'm afraid to expect good news.

10:45 a.m.

The CT scan was clear (CT stands for computerized [axial] tomography – CAT with the axial in it). My heart study showed no problems. I wish I felt happier than I do.

Dr. Stevens gave us 3 studies to read, so we could make our own judgement about the chemotherapy. After wading through the statistics (which I hardly trust anymore anyway) we've come to the conclusion that I should go through with the chemotherapy. The biggest danger is heart failure, which occurs in about 10% of patients getting Adriamycin (however, this 10% figure comes from a study in which 2 out of 20 patients total had heart failure). In this same study, 50% (of those 20 patients) had a ventricular abnormality that was asymptomatic but showed up on the tests. One wonders what such an abnormality might do after 10, 20, 40 years, since this study was conducted over a 4 year period. I guess one has to take one's chances in a case like this.

The study that was the most relevant to my case showed a dramatic difference with chemotherapy, especially in the case of synovial cell sarcomas (which is the full name of my little friend). Even so, there were

149

only 16 patients total with synovial cell sarcomas. 12 had chemo, 4 didn't. None of the 12 chemos had a recurrence, while 3 of the 4 non-chemos had recurrences, one of them ultimately dying. The statistics for all the other kinds of sarcomas weren't nearly as dramatic. But this is the only study in which patients with a synovial cell sarcoma were even treated (in the other study there were 3 who all fell in the non-chemo group) with chemotherapy. With results like that, I don't have much choice.

At the end of the paper on the study that was most relevant to me, there were some comments on how the patients tolerated the chemo. All of them lost their hair and all of them got it back. Most patients had moderate to severe nausea and vomiting in the first 12-24 hours after a treatment. The heart problems occurred. Permanent infertility occurred only when the chemo was combined with radiation to the pelvic area. In most patients under 35, the chemo alone depressed fertility temporarily but fertility recovered in most young patients after two years (they did 14 months of chemo instead of just 6).

There were some very grim statistics in these studies. The worst was that the overall 5 year survival rate for anyone with a grade III tumor (anywhere) is only 26%. But mention was made that treatment such as I have received improves that number to 40-60% (the surgery and the radiation with a linear accelerator especially). Then there were the statistics specific to me which predicted a 3 year survival rate of 92% with chemotherapy. So you can choose the ones you want to believe. I'll pick 92% and be optimistic. What else can I do? The idea of being cured and having a chance at having a baby is too sweet to ignore. And with a good attitude, it should be possible. Six months is not forever – and if I happen to be one of the 10% with heart failure, I guess I'm just a very unlucky person. If I'm lucky (and this is where I need to have a positive attitude, considering the last three months) I could be one of the 50% that don't have any damage to the heart.

One thing in these studies that I think is significant, is that people who had limbs amputated had worse results in either category than did those who had conservative surgery like I did. I attribute this partially to the emotional trauma of losing a limb – I think this shows that emotional factors do make a difference in whether or not the cancer recurs or eventually kills a person.

So. Regardless of how terrible I may feel right now, I can't afford to wallow in bitterness or self-pity. That could cost me my life.

Dr. Stevens said that if I want to go ahead with chemo, he wants me to have a permanent catheter installed (Vicki has one). That way they can give me IV's and draw blood without sticking me all the time. This does require surgery though (not again!) and I'll have to keep it clean. He also wants to try the cold cap for hair loss. And my heart will be closely monitored (although in the studies the heart failure occurred after the chemo was over).

Yesterday we went to Chi Chi's with my parents and Oma. When we got there, I could hear a baby crying in the bathroom and there was a bottle sitting on one of the benches. I had a hard time not crying. It's the unexpected things that get to you.

Friday, March 7, 1986

A.D. 13 weeks, 1 day

8:00 am.

Gwynne would've been two weeks old today. And we would have been the proudest and happiest parents. We keep getting cards for another Mrs. David Edwards who delivered the same day I did, who had a daughter and named her Elizabeth Ann. I can't believe in a God who could be this cruel.

It has only been two weeks and already we're back in the eye of the cancer hurricane, the fear for my life so strong you can taste it. It overrides the grief. I don't want it to be that way, but when I think about how fast it killed some people, I get really frightened. I want so much to get cured, to have a possibility to have a family, to celebrate my 30th birthday. After losing the baby I wanted more than anything in the world, I'm afraid I'll lose everything that I really want.

I need strength and hope and I have such a tenuous hold on them.

Saturday, March 8, 1986

A.D. 13 weeks, 2 days

9:00 a.m.

Once again I've been awake since before 8 a.m. As soon as I wake up even slightly, the events of February 21 start replaying themselves in my mind. I see myself in the recovery room telling Dave to go see Gwynne because she needs him more than I do, listening to all the other families with babies in the recovery room. I see us in my room waiting anxiously for news about our beautiful baby, and finally Dr. Brown coming in to say they'd done everything they could and it didn't look like she would make it. And me asking, "Is there a chance she won't die?" and the reply, "Where there's life, there's hope ..." We had so much hope. I miss her so much.

Tuesday, March 11, 1986

A.D. 13 weeks, 5 days

12:00 p.m.

Dave and I feel like we're in a tiny rubber raft in the middle of a stormy sea. We're constantly in fear of drowning or being engulfed by tidal waves. Every once in a while, it calms down and we get a care package from someone, but it never lasts long enough to get out of the storm.

Every little ache either one of us gets could mean disaster. We're constantly afraid of losing each other, since we've lost the baby we loved so much. We may never have another disaster again, but will we ever dare feel safe from them?

I feel drowned in sadness. I feel like I'm in a deep dark pit that I can't get out of by myself. Where is this all leading us? To ultimate happiness? Or to doom?

A.D. 13 weeks, 6 days

11:00 p.m.

And now I've had enough! Today we found out Dave has a cyst on his thyroid gland, I have arthritis in my wrist, and we had to take Cookie to the vet and leave her there to be operated on in the morning. That's the hardest thing – losing her would hurt a lot. She apparently swallowed a four foot piece of twine that I foolishly left lying around Monday night. Yesterday she was moping around and we found some runny vomit in various places. Today was worse – the vomit was bloody and she hadn't eaten at all as far as we could tell. So we took her temperature. The thermometer came out all bloody. She trusts us so much that she didn't even panic in the vet's office. He told us that in the worst case they would have to remove so much intestine that she would have to eat every 10-15 minutes just to stay alive. That would be unfair to her. He said in eight years he'd only had one cat with that bad of a problem. I didn't even want to hear it. So tomorrow he's going to cut the string into pieces, and gently pull it out. Poor Cookie! Stupid Cookie for eating string! Stupid me for leaving it lying around. Shit!

So what about Dave's cyst and my arthritis? Well, Dave has had pain in his neck since Sunday and could feel a lump there, so naturally we panicked and he went to the doctor today. Apparently it's not too worrisome – many people have them (if it's what they think it is) and they fill up with fluid when an infection is present, and then they go away. So hopefully it's not serious – just a pain in Dave's neck.

My wrist started hurting Monday after I spent the day typing. I was writing an article about the baby's death because I thought I might feel better. I cried a lot as I wrote it and felt decidedly worse for the next three days. But at least it's all on paper and I don't have to write it in my head anymore. Anyway, since it was my right hand, naturally I got worried, so today while I saw Dr. Himes I also talked to Dr. Macintyre and she looked at it and ordered and X-ray. She called me tonight to say there were no obvious soft-tissue masses in my wrist (which is what I cared about) but there was evidence of arthritis. Arthritis simply means inflammation of a joint – it does not necessarily have to be a debilitating condition. However, I've had this pain before ...

It was difficult going for my first post-partum exam – we walked in the door and the first thing we saw was a woman holding a new baby. More babies came and went, and a few pregnant women were in front of me. At least all the nurses knew and were sympathetic. I talked to Dr. Himes for a long time. Apparently this damn beta-streptococcus bacterium is a sneaky killer. They've been unable to detect a cause and effect – many more women carry it than infect their baby with it, and studies have shown no way to predict when it will strike or how to prevent it from happening. And with beta-strep it's possible that the infection started with the rupturing of the membranes and was as devastating as it was within twelve hours. But had I just gone in for a C-Section, it could still have gotten to her – it was found in my blood as well as the placenta. My poor baby just never stood a chance. And the statistics... one out of a thousand babies is lost to this infection – the old 0.1% again. At Magee, they lose 5 babies a year to it and they have 11,000 deliveries a year (the 1/1000 figure is nationwide). It was apparent that this infection is a real frustration to doctors. Dr. Himes sure seemed frustrated. Dr. Macintyre told me that any baby less than 2 months old who gets infected by the beta-strep bacteria is highly likely to die within 12-24 hours. God, what a tragedy!

Dr. Himes said that during my next pregnancy he'll monitor me carefully and if he sees any beta-strep bacteria, he's going to treat me aggressively, even though there's no proven method of treatment. He said that I could safely get pregnant in 3-4 months if cancer weren't a consideration – so whenever we want to try after the chemo is over we can go right ahead. One ray of hope in an otherwise bleak and gloomy outlook.

The vet's bill for Cookie is going to be anywhere from $100-200. The timing is just unbelievable! It'll be worth it if she's just all right. Please, let something go right for a change!

The catheter is going to be implanted on Monday. I get out of the hospital, Cookie goes in. Cookie gets out, I go in. I get out...?

11:20 a.m.

Cookie is being operated on right now. The vet didn't sound like she was in great danger, though, so we just have to be optimistic and believe everything's alright. Yesterday they couldn't find proof that she had a string in her, but she still wasn't right. Today she refused to eat, which means there's definitely something wrong. But she's perky and sitting up and meowing, so she's in good shape to withstand surgery. The vet thinks maybe because the string is so thick and made of plastic, it's working its way through the intestines without cutting them. Everyone else is worried, but I'm not. I'm past worrying by now. She just has to be okay.

It's three weeks since the baby died. I think we're starting to adjust. Just being alive doesn't hurt anymore – the moments of pain are interspersed with moments of "normal" life. We still think about her most of the time, but at least I'm not constantly crying.

Saturday, March 15, 1986

A.D. 14 weeks, 2 days

10:00 a.m.

There was no string in Cookie's gut. She did have
enlarged lymph nodes. The vet told me that she could
possibly have feline leukemia virus, which works a lot
like AIDS, suppressing the immune system. If that was
it, the enlarged lymph nodes could mean lymphatic
sarcoma. I almost died when he said that. He took out a
node to be biopsied. He also did a blood test for the
leukemia virus and that came back negative last night.
So the likelihood of sarcoma is low. Chances are the
lymph nodes are swollen because she has some general
infection. We're going to visit her today. Yesterday we
were so depressed waiting to hear if we'd have to put her
to sleep (a nice way of saying "put her to death"). She's
still not out of the woods, but at least she's alive after the
surgery.

Monday, March 17, 1986

A.D. 14 weeks, 4 days

4:00 p.m.

The Cook is back! The vet is very embarrassed because yesterday she passed the string, so it was in there after all. Embarrassment aside, they did present us with a bill for $325 (even though he said, "she got better in spite of us"). It's hard to complain – we're so happy to have Cookie back alive and purring that we don't really care about the money. All the individual items on the bill seem reasonable enough – the final price is just hard to swallow, especially when they didn't end up being the ones to cure her. Oh well, what's money when you've got your favorite pet back in one piece?

I got the catheter put in today. It's a Hickman catheter. It was more painful than I expected. I hate surgery. I hate general anesthesia because I don't believe I'll wake up, and I hate local because it always hurts. I'm tired of being in pain. I start chemotherapy on Wednesday.

3:45 p.m.

Leslee had another boy. Both she and the baby are doing fine. How I wish that could have been said about me and Gwynne three weeks ago! I will certainly never take a baby for granted after all this. I'm glad I have an excuse not to visit her at the hospital – it would be too painful. I can't stand going to buy baby clothes for her either. I'm sure she'll understand. I'm glad for her. But I'm envious, too. She already has one – why couldn't I keep my one baby?

Mom just hypnotized me in preparation for the chemo. I didn't come out of it feeling good – I had three imaginary battles with cancer cells in my lungs. It was frightening to admit they might be there already. It makes me more anxious to go through with the chemo. Was my imagination preparing me for the worst? Or was my body informing me that I still haven't won? At least the battles were satisfying – I imagined beating up the cancer cells with fists and clubs – a whole gang against one, just overpowering it. Even in a trance I could feel the anger and it was good to take it out on a deserving culprit. Just thinking about that makes me feel better.

Mom also had me imagine lying on a beach with the sun warming my body, the white light from the sun containing all the love from my parents, Dave, my brother and sister, and my little girl; all the love I gave my baby returning to me through this light. This made me cry (and still does). I've been feeling relatively calm lately, but I guess I still have all of these emotions really close to the surface. It's nice to think of her love returning to me. There's still so much pain.

The care of the catheter is a bigger hassle than I expected. The surgery to put it in wasn't just a little slice – it took almost two hours. He had to make a cut below my collar bone (left this time, since I was tired of my right shoulder hurting). Then he had to dig around in there for the cephalic vein, which in my case was down <u>deep</u> and small to boot. Then he had to tunnel under the skin between my breasts. There he made a smaller incision and the catheter was pulled up through the tunnel. Then he had to put the catheter in my vein and thread it to the superior vena cava, the vein that goes into the heart. That part didn't hurt, but it took a long time because it was difficult to see the catheter on the fluoroscope (or whatever they used) without contrast dye (to which, I had to tell them, I was allergic). So they had to call in a radiologist and wait for him to scrub up, etc. It was all a lot more complicated than I expected. And now the cleaning ritual takes about an hour, although I expect it'll go faster after the wounds heal and I've had some practice. It's disgusting to see a white plastic tube come out of your body. It makes you feel more like you're really sick, especially because it's about 10" long and forked, with clamps on each "lumen" (fork), so it's not easy to hide.

Wednesday, March 19, 1986

A.D. 14 weeks, 6 days

10:00 p.m.

Cookie's not completely well yet; neither am I. No chemotherapy after all today. I have a sore throat and a fever. How convenient. I did that before I got my wisdom teeth out, but I went ahead with that anyway. The doctor wouldn't let me go ahead with the chemo. I hardly ever get a fever. It's amazing that I'd get one now.

We're concerned about Cookie again. She acts like she's in more pain and she won't eat. We called the vet again and he said we should only feed her mushy baby food – dry food could irritate her intestines. She threw up a giant hairball today, too. The vet said that could make her act sicker. He said we shouldn't worry unless she gets very depressed, but we can't help it.

Dave keeps telling Cookie how much he loves her. I think both of us are transferring the love we were saving for the baby to Cookie – and also the concern.

I can't wait till all of this is over and we can live a normal life again! That's making the assumption that I'll be cured and it'll be possible to live a normal life. Dave said to me that he wondered if he would crack under the pressure. I've been wondering that myself. I need so much care right now and I depend on him for it all.

Having to force pills down Cookie's throat and worrying about taking her to the vet is just more than he can take. On the one hand he tells me not to do things so I won't hurt myself, but on the other he expresses resentment over having to do everything. And since it's very difficult for me to let things be done for me anyway (except cooking), it makes me feel doubly helpless, dependent and unhappy. I wonder if things will ever get better for us. It would be so nice for us to have the family we dreamed of and live peacefully in our little house. I wonder if we'll ever get that lucky?

Friday, March 21, 1986

A.D. 15 weeks, 1 day

5:30 p.m.

Another of those unexpected things: there was a woman in the grocery store today who had a little baby in her cart. The baby was sleeping peacefully and looked like it was about the age Gwynne would be now – four weeks already. The baby had the same pout Gwynne had – it made me cry in the middle of the Giant Eagle. I still feel so angry and sad that other people have babies and no cancer and I lost my baby that I wanted so much! It's not fair that it should all happen to us! I want my baby.

Sunday, March 23, 1986

A.D. 15 weeks, 3 days

11:00 a.m.

Oma left today. It's starting to feel lonely around here
again. I'll miss her; I'm glad she was here for the funeral
and to keep us company.

Cookie seems to be all better – she's out hunting
again. I wish I could say the same for me. My shoulder
aches all the time. And I feel fat but totally disinclined to
do anything about it. I just want to be pregnant.

Monday, March 24, 1986

A.D. 15 weeks, 4 days

9:30 a.m.

In my Freshman Spanish class, I made friends with a man who was 76 years old. He was taking Spanish and Portuguese because he was finally going to make the trip to Europe that he'd always dreamed of. What if he didn't make it? Is it sad that he never realized his dream, or is it good that he still had a dream when he died?

Tuesday, March 25, 1986

A.D. 15 weeks, 5 days

9:00 p.m.

Chemotherapy is awful. I was up all night throwing up and I still feel queasy. I don't know if I can stand this. It feels so unnatural and unhealthy. I wish I could go to sleep for six months and get this over with. Yuk.

Friday, March 28, 1986

A.D. 16 weeks, 1 day

5:30 p.m.

It's been five weeks since the baby died. She should have been born about now. We drove to the cemetery today and her headstone still isn't there. Her grave is hard to distinguish now and I would feel so much better if the marker were there. I just received a call from the wife of the stoneworker, who says it might be up to a month before the cemetery gets the foundation in. I don't feel like our job as parents is finished yet.

Mom and I had a good hypnosis session last night and now I feel much better. Even yesterday I was feeling nauseated and tired. I was also having trouble sleeping, and since I went back to work on Wednesday, that didn't help my physical condition. Now at least I slept all night and I feel almost normal. This hypnosis is really a good thing – very calming.

7:40 a.m.

We had the most horrible fight of our life together last night. It was really frightening. I started it by getting mad when Dave smoked a couple of cigarettes (he quit about 1-1/2 years ago). I tried to stop myself from getting angry, but another part of me really wanted to go crazy. We argued back and forth about the smoking – I wanted him to say he'd never touch a cigarette again and he wouldn't say it. I told him I didn't want him to do anything known to cause cancer and he told me that it was no guarantee and besides, smoking a couple of cigarettes couldn't possibly kill him. But he was so hard and distant – I just had to get to him. So I kept sitting and staring at him and telling him to do it for me and he finally started yelling, "What do you want from me? Leave me alone, dammit, leave me alone!" and finally he pushed me into the door, still yelling for me to leave him alone, and threw a pillow at me. Hard. I went into the dark living room and cried on the couch and listened to him ranting in the bedroom – "just three lousy drags on two cigarettes – I counted them and she drives me to the breaking point – why can't she leave me alone – egging me on until I can't take anymore – I've got to get out of here!"

171

When I heard that I got really scared and ran back into the bedroom where he was putting his pants on to go – and I cried, "Don't leave me! Please don't leave me! I'm so sorry, it's all my fault, please forgive me, I'm really sorry, please don't go!" And he sat on the edge of the bed and said in anguish, "I've got nowhere to go. I've got <u>nowhere</u> to go!" He went into the living room and laid down on the couch and kept making sounds like he was choking to death and just repeated over and over, "We are all alone … choke ... I am all alone ... gag … I've got nowhere to go … there is good and there is evil ... but there's no God ... it hurts so much to be all alone..."

I thought I'd lost him. I sat next to him and just touched him and thought to myself that I would have to find him a mental hospital. And I thought I could handle that, too. I can handle anything. And that in itself is very frightening.

After a while Dave started coming back – he started to sound normal again – "You know when I told you that I was near the breaking point? Well, I've been a few steps away from it now – I could see it so very clearly – it's so easy to lose your mind." Slowly he got himself back together and started to tell me how much he loved me. That was what had frightened me the most, was the thought that he might leave me and take his love away from me. Because even though I thought I could handle it, I also knew it could kill me. And once Dave was himself again, I realized that I knew <u>exactly</u> what he was saying – we are, ultimately, completely alone with ourselves and we can't escape from ourselves. Only I've been aware of it slowly but surely over the past few months, instead of realizing it in one fell swoop.

Well, we made up and made love and clung to each other, red-eyed and desperate. We've been through hell and it's not over yet. Dave hadn't cried since three days after Gwynne died and I really think last night was just the dam breaking and all his fears and agonies tumbling out at once (he doesn't seem to be so sure of that, though). I'm glad it happened because he's been so frighteningly calm in the face of all this. I just hope he doesn't build another mental dam – I hope he can start expressing his fears when he feels them and then get them over with. But I may be asking for the impossible. I'll just be happy if we get back to "normal".

Monday, March 31, 1986

A.D. 16 weeks, 4 days

9:20 p.m.

The last few days have been absolutely gorgeous – blue, cloudless skies, 75-80 degrees, warm breezes. I couldn't ask for more perfect weather. This weather makes us feel like everything might be all right after all.

Yesterday we were very close after the fight. Dave said something just "snapped" inside him, but he was completely himself by morning. We talked about it and then decided to enjoy the day, so we went to my parents' house and hung out on the deck, then went to Dave's parents' house and had a great Easter dinner.

Today at work I felt good, really good. I got into work, I didn't get sleepy, and I was happy to see everyone again. A lot of people said it was so nice to have me back because I smile all the time. Isn't it amazing? I go through all this and still I'm the one that makes everyone smile back at me. Sometimes I think I'm a very special person. It sounds conceited, but I don't think it hurts to value yourself. Besides, it makes it that much more important to work on saving your own life.

Even though I'm starting to feel happy, there are still many times when tears sting my eyes for my little Gwynne. I stare at her picture almost every day. She was so lovely! And every day I wonder why I had to go through losing her. I see other people with babies and wonder what twist of fate could make their baby live and mine die. It's a never-ending torment for people who lose their babies.

I still feel calm from the last hypnosis session. Thank God I have my mother!

Tuesday, April 1, 1986

A.D. 16 weeks, 5 days

10:00 p.m.

I was talking to Kathy (the secretary who is pregnant) today and she said she would have to sell her car because with the baby corning she couldn't afford it anymore. It struck me that even though I was talking to her about her baby, I was thinking that she wouldn't really have a baby – like me. I think of pregnant women as people who aren't necessarily going to end up with a baby. I have trouble understanding why they say certain things until I realize they're planning on the presence of their baby, much like we were only six weeks ago. I wonder if that will ever go away?

Friday, April 4, 1986

A.D. 17 weeks, 1 day

Fridays are so hard. I feel so sad. Something always happens to remind me of Gwynne on a Friday. Six weeks. I miss her so much.

The autopsy report is back. We have a tentative appointment on Monday to discuss it with Dr. Brown. God, I hope we won't have any more cause to be sad for a long time. I'm so tired of feeling sad and scared.

7:40 p.m.

We didn't have the appointment yet. It's going to be on Friday at 4:00 p.m. Thinking about the NICU made me feel sad again. I miss my baby so much!

I went to Leslee's house on Sunday and held Shane for a while. He weighs almost nine pounds and he seemed so small. Imagine how little Gwynne was. Life seems to be back the way it was before I found the lump, except I feel ten years older, wiser, and sadder. I feel like I'll be too old to have another baby in six months – I feel like I'm aging at the rate of two years each month. It's almost inconceivable that only 5-1/2 months ago our biggest worry was whether we'd get our mortgage or not. It has to be longer than that! I can hardly remember past then.

Sally Turnbull (she and her family have been friends of our family ever since we moved to Pittsburgh in 1975) brought over a needlepoint frame for the picture of Gwynne. She needle-pointed Gwynne's name, birthdate and weight on it along with booties and a border of pink hearts. It's very pretty and it's wonderful to have something so personal for Gwynne's picture. Sally also brought a book, "Living With Cancer", which has a Christian perspective. I read the book and it struck me how all the people said they felt calm after they had accepted Jesus Christ as their Savior. It struck me because I've been feeling so calm all along. I feel like I can handle anything and I'm not really afraid of dying. Although right now dying is still abstract it's certainly not right around the corner as it was for these people. At any rate, I feel at peace with God — even with all the terrible things that have happened. I feel lucky in what I have and happy to be alive. I don't know if I'll keep feeling this way if things go really badly, but for now at least I'm calm. And I know Gwynne's soul went to a place where she's loved and cherished, and that's where I'll go too. This doesn't come from any religion – it comes from deep inside of me.

Tuesday, April 8, 1986

A.D. 17 weeks, 5 days

7:10 p.m.

My hair is starting to fall out. Every time I run my hand through it, 10-20 hairs come out too. My only consolation is that the grey ones come out too. If it has to happen, I hope it goes fast. I hate wondering when I'll be too bald to go without a wig.

Wednesday, April 9, 1986

A.D. 17 weeks, 6 days

9:30 a.m.

I still have hair. It wasn't all on my pillow when I woke up this morning.

I saw Dr. Himes and Dr. Macintyre today. Dr. Himes told me he's changing jobs. I knew this would happen to me – I find a doctor I really like, and he transfers out of the HMO. I wish I could defect with him. He told me he was telling only the patients he felt close to about his leaving.

We talked about the baby's infection a little more and he said that this was the worst tragedy he'd encountered as a doctor; that this had gotten to him as much as the first time he encountered death. This is just why I like him so much – he talks to me honestly and openly and isn't afraid to show he's a human being.

He asked me how Dave was and I told him that I wasn't sure because he's not talking much about how he feels and I can't tell if it's because he's not feeling much or because he's holding it in. Dr. Himes said that he got the impression that Dave was a silent type from the way he was in the hospital, and he thought there must still be a lot of things to work through. He said if he were in the same position, he would expect to have them anyhow. At that point I asked him if he was married and he looked embarrassed and said, "No," and I said, "Not enough time, huh?" and he said, "No, that's not it." Well, I hope he has <u>someone.</u> He's too nice to be lonely. (In going through all this I place a tremendous value on having someone to love and to talk to). At any rate, as he was leaving the room I said I wished he weren't leaving and he came back in, closed the door and said, "This shouldn't go out of this room, but there may be an arrangement," and then he told me how the HMO had trouble assigning OB/GYN's to the North Hills so his group might be used to cover the North Hills area if no other doctor is willing to transfer. I hope it works out that way – I can't possibly change plans now, and I like him so much.

Dr. Macintyre, was also concerned about Dave. She didn't have any suggestions though, just friendly concern. She did say that many women lose some hair after having babies (Barb said the same thing), and many people don't lose it from chemo, so not to give up hope yet.

Everybody keeps saying "You look good". I guess it was worth my depression last Friday trying on all these clothes and feeling fat and ugly in all of them, to find some (finally) that get people to tell me how nice I look. Twenty-five pounds is a lot to lose, but I don't have to look bad while I'm losing it. I've been exercising every day and I'm starting to feel better.

Dave and I had a talk tonight about dying and God. He said sometimes it hits him what it would be like to lose me, and he feels depressed about it often. He repeated "We are all alone" again. I told him what I think about God — God is not a being or creature, but a spirit, maybe a collective spirit, that we all aspire to. God doesn't need us but simply is. And the joy you feel on a warm spring day when everything is beautiful and it feels good to be alive, at that moment you're closer to God than in everyday life. When you die, you enter that feeling forever. I've been feeling close to God very often lately, very much at peace, and I wish I could transfer that to Dave. But it seems that he's not ready for it – after all, I'm the one that would die and leave him alone. Maybe it even frightens him that I would think of death as something positive, even though I have every intention of staying alive (I think we were meant to love life more than anything – dying is natural and good, but not to be rushed into any more than being born), Anyhow, I wish Dave were with me in my little peaceful circle, because I'm sure he could use some peace himself.

11:00 a.m.

We met with Dr. Brown yesterday. The autopsy report wasn't back yet, but he just wanted to talk to us and make sure we didn't have any unanswered questions. He said he'd call us if there is anything surprising in the autopsy finding but he's pretty sure there won't be any surprises. The social worker told us we could have a copy of the report if we want it. I don't know if we do. It was hard to go, but Dr. Brown is a very nice guy and it was calming to talk with him. He asked us to let him know if I get pregnant again.

My hair is driving me crazy. It's falling out in handfuls, there's still enough left to go without a wig but there's hair all over the place. I'm tempted to shave it all off, but I haven't reached the breaking point yet. It's very depressing to find a major percentage of your hair in the bottom of the tub after a shower, but it's kind of interesting to think of myself as hairless – strange but interesting (it's not just the hair on my head either).

Back to Dr. Brown. We asked mostly what could be done (and what could have been done) to prevent this infection. It's pretty obvious that there's not much. He told us that he had had one case where twins were delivered by C-section with intact membranes and one of the twins got the infection and died while the other didn't. One thing he was speculating on was whether I had any antibodies to the strep at the time. He thought maybe I didn't and so I didn't pass any on to the baby. He said I should ask my doctor if I have antibodies to the strep now (even though it would be really surprising if I didn't). My cancer and the radiation are most likely totally unrelated. It just boggles the mind that in 4 months two extremely rare things should happen to me. Maybe I should play the lottery.

Sunday, April 13, 1986

A.D. 18 weeks, 3 days

My hair was so thin and fuzzy today that I had to wear a wig. Patches of scalp were showing through. In the morning Dave cut off the longer hair in the back. Then we went to Mom and Dad's and Mom and I went to her office for a hypnosis session. Afterward I decided that I'd rather be the one in control of the hair loss, so I had Mom cut it really, short and then shave it off. There was still a lot left, but at least now I don't have to dig it out of the tub and find it all over my pillow. It's not as bad as I expected. But I don't have to look at it – Dave does. He doesn't seem to mind, though. When Leslee and Mike came over they didn't even notice I had my wig on. So now if I can only stand the heat and the itching.

I was drawn to the cemetery yesterday. I stopped by Gwynne's grave and was struck by how tiny it was. I cried for my baby once again.

Tuesday, April 15, 1986

A.D. 18 weeks, 5 days

8:30 p.m.

Last night U.S. forces attacked Libya. It was an attempt to show terrorists what they can expect if they keep up bombing planes, but we're afraid they won't be stopped by this. All I can think of is that they killed Gaddafi's baby daughter in the air raid, and does that make us any better than them? There must be a better way...

My wig is a good one – I keep getting compliments on my new hairstyle. I kind of like my almost bald head except for the temperature – it's very sensitive to the cold. Dad said on Sunday, when he saw my wig, that he had to be careful that he didn't start loving me more in my wig than in my real hair. That's just about the nicest thing someone could say about it.

We both have been thinking about the baby a lot. It just seems so incredible that we had a daughter and now we don't. It's so bewildering. I thought the pain was going away, but it was just ebbing for a while.

Sunday, April 20, 1986

A.D. 19 weeks, 3 days

8:00 a.m.

I believe I'm back in the world of the living. I had my treatment on Friday and I didn't get sick at all. But the stuff they gave me to keep me from getting sick made me extremely sleepy and lethargic. Today I'm going to try not taking that stuff and see if I feel any better.

We're trying a new way of eating — fruit only until noon, then vegetables and either carbohydrates or proteins, never mixing them. So not cutting anything out, just eating it at different times in the day. Terri says it's working for her.

Monday, April 21, 1986

A.D. 19 weeks, 4 days

5:30 p.m.

I had the most bizarre reaction to the drugs they gave me last night! I was taking Compazine – That's what kept me from getting sick at all – and then I switched to the Torecan I had left over from my last treatment. I took my last one at about 1 p.m. and by 6 p.m. my eyebrows kept knitting and I couldn't stop them. Then my head started forcing itself to the right and up, so my eyes were forced to look at the ceiling. This really frightened us. Dave called the HMO and they told us to go to the emergency room. Luckily Mom had phoned a few minutes earlier and recognized my symptoms as something very treatable that is a common side effect of this drug called an extrapyramidal reaction. So we went to the ER and while they were calling around to different doctors it just kept getting worse until my head was jerked all the way back and my arms and legs were trembling fiercely. I felt like crying – and Dave was in the waiting room. Then finally the nurse from the IV team that showed me how to take care of my catheter came down to show the ER nurse how to deal with my Hickman catheter. She gave me Benadryl and within minutes the symptoms were subsiding. After a second shot of Benadryl, they went away completely. Mom and Dad came and stayed. I am so lucky to have them! Mom knew all about the drug, so as long as she was around, I felt confident everything was going to be okay. As a psychologist, she's familiar with the psychotropic drugs some of her patients get prescribed by their psychiatrists. Apparently Torecan is one of those.

After we went home, I slept for about an hour and then woke up every 5-15 minutes to see if it was time to take more Benadryl because I did <u>not</u> want those symptoms to come back! So from 11 p.m. to 3 a.m. I was up constantly. This morning I tried sleeping in, but finally gave up and went to work. I feel better now.

Mom and Dad are going to Europe despite the danger of terrorist attacks. They're taking a Belgian airline so they feel fairly safe. I hope nothing happens to them. Last time they went I had to call and tell them I had cancer. I hope this time the trip will be uneventful. I'm afraid of losing them!

9:00 a.m.

Mom called me yesterday from Greece to let me know that she had arrived safely. I feel a lot better now. Now Dad has to get over and then they both have to get home again.

Gwynne's birth certificate arrived yesterday, bringing it all back once again. Proof that she once existed. I took one of the pictures of her to Fotomat to get copies made. When it comes back I'll get the other one copied and I'll always be able to have her picture close to me. I've had this urge to cut a bunch of the daffodils in our yard and put them on her grave. Maybe tomorrow.

I stopped by to see Dad last night after I got blood drawn (it took them four tries – it's about time they started to use the catheter). We had a very interesting conversation. He started out talking about a colleague at work who was in his early thirties and just buried his wife last week. She had been diagnosed as having cancer about a month after I was. She was 28. I started to talk about how <u>scary</u> cancer was because it's so sneaky – you can have it and not know it, and there's no known cause for it. Then Dad said he believed the cause was a multitude of things, like the way we eat, what we eat, but also internal things such as our emotional well-being. I said I used to believe that but I'd been so calm over the last few years so it didn't fit me. He replied that he thought a started long before that, or at least the atmosphere for the cancer to be allowed to start was probably a long time in the making. He mentioned folk sayings like the Dutch "he's eating himself up with worry" which is literally what happens when you get an ulcer. Then he thought a little about the word cancer – in Dutch "kanker" has another meaning which, loosely translated, means tying yourself up in knots. And revelation! That applies to my life before I met Dave and even for a few years after I met him. I was always having difficult emotional relationships and I would often be instrumental in complicating them. Only living with Dave softened me up and made me start to curb my sharp tongue – and feel more secure in being loved. That had always been at the bottom of my tangles – that I wasn't sure I was loved. Since I got the cancer, all of a sudden I <u>knew</u> how much I was loved and valued – everyone was forced to show it at once. The cancer actually changed my life for the better! I am a much calmer, happier, more serene and more loving person than I ever was before. And it's thanks to the cancer. Actually in the last few months I've been happier than ever before, even with the terrible ordeals I've had to face. Let's hope Dad was right about the emotional atmosphere of my body allowing the cancer to "tie me up in knots", because that means my body would be inhospitable to it now that I've changed, and I'll be able to enjoy my new emotional stability for many happy years!

One sad note – Max just told me that Vicki will have to stay away from her baby for four months while she undergoes the bone marrow transplant. How unbearable! What will that do to her emotional state? I haven't talked to her since my last radiation treatment. (I felt like I couldn't after losing Gwynne) but I'm ready to now. I wonder if there's anything I can do to help?

Dave and I have been vegetarian for over a week now. One day before last week I was eating a pork chop and cutting all the fat away from it and suddenly I thought "What have they done to this animal to make it get big enough for me to eat?" After that, I just couldn't stomach any more meat, with maybe the exception of fish and seafood, because even though we're polluting the waters of the earth, I have a feeling that the poisons aren't nearly as concentrated in them as in what's purposely being given to animals meant to be slaughtered. So far I feel great and have finally lost 3 pounds. I think this should make a difference to the cancer-atmosphere, too.

Sunday, April 27, 1986

A.D. 20 weeks, 3 days

7:40 p.m.

Friday we both felt sad. Dave went up in Gwynne's room and talked to her – he said it was so sunny and bright in there that it just felt like she had to be there. I cried for her again. I saw a picture of a father holding his baby and it made me so sad. We went to a party that night but I just kept feeling sad all evening. Saturday we took some flowers to her tiny grave. It was hot but the chestnut tree threw shade over her grave and made it just the right temperature. Her headstone still isn't there.

From there we went to a picnic. I played volleyball and did rather well despite my hot wig and jeans. I wish these 25 pounds would come off already! I don't have anything to wear. I've been eating right and exercising, but the fat just seems to like it on my hips and thighs.

We spent all of today mowing. Why did we buy this house?! I can't wait to get the tractor fixed. Half an acre was a chore. 1-1/3 acres is just too much.

My friend Dave Young called from Ohio today. I just sent him a letter telling him everything – the last time we talked was right before I found the lump. Hopefully he and his wife are coming to Pittsburgh soon so we can visit.

7:20 a.m.

Whenever we think about the baby, we both see her more as a wise, serious little old lady than as a little baby with waving arms and legs and a toothless grin. We never saw her any other way. I wonder if we'll ever stop thinking about her? I don't think so. We loved her so much and had so many plans for her. I still feel so sad so often.

Dad flew to Europe yesterday on Pan Am because his flight was cancelled. Apparently he made it – I haven't heard any news flashes about planes being bombed. He stopped in New York to see Hugo and tell him that he's being sued. Just what our family needs right now. Hugo hit a jogger – or the jogger hit him – last November and even though the guy was able to get up on his own and was released from the hospital within two hours, he's claiming serious internal injuries – worth $600,000! Hugo said it was dark, the guy had dark clothes on, and he never saw him even though he looked twice. The suit is claiming he was "careless, negligent and wantonly reckless". This when he was the one that called the police and ambulance. Hugo says he stopped at the stop sign, looked both ways, saw nothing and pulled into the intersection. In the middle of the intersection he heard a big thump on the left fender and slammed on the brakes to find this guy rolling on the ground. He found a hand print on the hood later – the guy could have just smacked the hood and faked an injury just so he could sue. Poor Hugo – he's such a nice guy to be screwed like this!

7:00 a.m.

This morning as I was jumping on my mini trampoline, I felt a jolt as I remembered what I dreamed last night: I had the baby in my arms. I knew she was going to die, but I was holding her and kissing and cuddling her and as I put my hand on her tummy I could feel her! I wish I could have done that before she died. I wish she could have died in my arms, feeling my love and my heartbeat, not surrounded by strangers and machines. When I die, I want to die in the arms of someone I love.

It's ten weeks today but I can still see and feel the events of February 21st as clear as day. It hurts so much.

Saturday, May 3, 1986

A.D. 21 weeks, 2 days

9:10 a.m.

I found out yesterday that one of my single friends is pregnant and plans to have an abortion. It makes me feel really sad – it reminds me of just how much I wanted my baby. I can see the point of view of the Right to Lifers – but even 8-1/2 hours of parenthood taught me how much of a responsibility a child is – and how much of a burden. There's nothing worse than an unwanted baby. So I support her decision, but it still reminds me of how much I'd like to be pregnant and growing another beautiful baby. The last two days I've felt so sad and missed Gwynne so much. I think I'll go lay some more flowers on her grave.

I miss my parents. They'll be back in about 10 days but I wish it was sooner.

Yesterday a bill arrived for two chest X-rays for "baby female Edwards". Somehow I feel like we shouldn't have to think about those bills since she died. The bill contributed greatly to my sadness. I got Gwynne's picture back from Fotomat and put it in the frame Mrs. Turnbull gave us. I hung it in the living room. It looks so sweet (and sad).

Wednesday, May 7, 1986

A.D. 21 weeks, 6 days

10:20 a.m.

I got a fever last night. In the middle of the night it hit 101 degrees. I'm staying home from work today but my fever is relatively low – 99 degrees. I wonder if I should call the doctor? I wonder what's wrong with me – I don't feel bad except for sore muscles and no appetite. I wish my Mom were here!

I've been feeling frightened lately – things have been too calm; something must be working on going wrong. I've been thinking about heart failure. That's pretty horrible – your heart becomes incapable of pumping all the blood in your body, so it backs up. Your lungs fill with fluid and your feet swell. You literally drown in your own blood. It can sometimes be controlled with drugs, but it seems like a horrible way to live. I guess you might become a candidate for a heart transplant then.

So many things could go wrong – and kill me. Or make it impossible to live normally and have a baby. I'm looking for assurances that just don't exist.

Friday, May 9, 1986

A.D. 22 weeks, 1 day

6:00 p.m.

Another Friday. Sigh ... I put the baby's picture on my desk in a beautiful little octagonal frame. I'm so sad that I don't get to be her Mommy. Mother's Day is Sunday and I want to be honored as a mother but I don't think anyone will – except Dave, who pointed out that I was eligible for Mother's Day just like he is for Father's Day. That little face on my desk reminds me of how much I love her and how much I miss her. I envy every parent in the world. But I don't want their children. I want mine. I can't wait until all of this is over so we can have another baby. I hope and pray that it will all be over soon.

Tuesday, May 13, 1986

A.D. 22 weeks, 5 days

11:30 pm.

I'm not writing as often anymore – I must be having fewer attacks of self-pity or hopelessness (that's when I usually write).

Lately, I've been feeling like I have the corner on the market of unhappiness – I have very low tolerance for other peoples' pain. I keep wanting to say, "You think that's bad? Look what happened to me!" But I'm really so lucky in so many ways – I have a wonderful husband and we're very much in love, both our families are warm, loving and supportive, I have a good job that pays well enough to have a decent house, car and furniture, I have financial security (except for the short-term disability), we have a ton of friends and all kinds of social engagements (which is why I never have time to write anymore). But we also have a room upstairs full of baby things, freshly painted with ducks marching along one wall – we didn't have time to put them on the other wall before I went in the hospital – and a bassinet for which I made a new white lace skirt. That bassinet in which I can still so clearly see a tiny baby sleeping on her tummy with a finger in her mouth. It's hard to believe that she was never really in there.

It's scary to think how much I wanted Gwynne and how easily she was taken away from me. That's how much I want to live and have another baby to love. Will that be taken from me too? Or worse yet, could I become less and less healthy, so living a fulfilling life would be more and more difficult, so people would have to take care of me? I can imagine nothing worse. And yet – it has happened to other people; it could certainly happen to me.

You'd think from reading this that I'm sad all the time. But that's not true — we had a great weekend and we have plans for the next four weekends. We put the boat in the water (Dave's parents' sailboat) on Sunday and spent a beautiful day with them and Dave's been working on our new deck while I sew like crazy on my dress for Sue's wedding on Saturday. We're too busy to be sad. Except at night.

Mom's coming home tomorrow! She's back in the States! And Dave got me a Mother's Day card – how sweet!

10:30 p.m.

I'm 26 today. I made it! Let's hope I make it to 62. I went to my appointment with Dr. Johnson today and everything seems to be fine. He said I wasn't getting a high enough dosage of Adriamycin to really worry about heart problems, and that the ovaries of young people (including myself) were usually strong enough not to be harmed by chemotherapy. I liked him better this time. He's not going to give me any prescriptions for nausea this time since I didn't get sick at all last time. He said if I wanted to smoke pot I should do it before my next treatment to have it in my system. My next treatment is Monday. He said that my scar from the catheter might be sore because the Adriamycin affects scar tissue. His scale said I lost 6-1/2 pounds!

I went shopping with Mom and Nicolette all afternoon and spent the $100 Dave's parents gave me. I got many clothes – most of them will fit me as I shrink. We went out to dinner at our favorite restaurant and got our favorite waiter. There was a tense moment when he asked about the baby, since we'd seen him a week before she was born, but after that we had a nice time.

People are generous when you have cancer – too bad I can't take it all with me. But I won't need to – I'll be around to watch the clothes I bought and received today come back in style.

I still haven't finished my dress for the wedding. I don't know when I will – the idea behind taking a day off was to finish it, but that just didn't work out. Oh well – one way or another it'll get done.

I read an article in a magazine written by a man about how his baby boy died. It was very similar to our story – down to her having to be wheeled to the NICU to see the baby before he died. Only she made it so he could die in her arms. If he can sell his story, I should be able to sell mine.

Monday, May 19, 1986

A.D. 23 weeks, 4 days

9:23 a.m.

I'm getting ready to go to my next treatment. I hope I won't get sick or weak.

The wedding was fun. Sue and Rick looked so happy! I finished my dress at 4:30 a.m. the night before the wedding. They're in Bermuda now, those lucky devils! I can't wait to take a vacation!

I keep thinking and planning that things will be all right, but every once in a while it occurs to me how bad it would be if I had a recurrence – more surgery, more radiation, more chemotherapy – if it's treatable. I just have to stay free of it.

Tuesday, May 20, 1986

A.D. 23 weeks, 5 days

10:00 p.m.

Chemotherapy this time was a breeze. Dr. Johnson didn't give me any prescriptions – just the drugs they gave with the chemotherapy. And I didn't throw up! I even went to work for a half day today! Lucky me!

Those 6-1/2 pounds I lost at Dr. Johnson's office were almost all back on by yesterday. Too much birthday and wedding cake. Today it was back to the old grindstone.

Thursday, May 22, 1986

A.D. 24 weeks

7:15 a.m.

I've been feeling negative lately. It's time for another hypnosis session. I keep thinking about tumors in my lungs and what that would mean. I've got to be positive! I have from 60-100% chance to be cured depending on which study you use. But I'm still scared. I want to grow old with Dave. I don't want to have cancer anymore.

Sunday, May 25, 1986

A.D. 24 weeks, 3 days

Friday Dr. Macintyre called me to set up a meeting with a bunch of nurses to train them on how to draw blood from the catheter. The last time I went in to have blood drawn, she had to do it – no one else would try because my veins were so small and deep. So I won't have to be stuck anymore.

Friday evening Mom and I had a long hypnosis session. I was really anxious before the session and afterwards I was a lot calmer. It really does help. Mom is very good at picking out points from our conversation and turning them into images to use during the hypnosis. We talked for about an hour before doing the hypnoses and we both cried. It's still so sad what I've gone through. I get so upset when I see other babies, especially if their parents don't appreciate them enough. And I was really getting worried about getting a recurrence – things have been too calm since the baby died. I felt like I could never be lucky enough to live a normal life with children. And maybe I won't be, but maybe I will and it's important not to give the cancer a chance to come back. I've also been very angry at the way it disrupted my life — I'm tired of caring for the catheter every day and of being bald. I want my hair back! I want to go swimming in a creek! The hypnosis got me back to a calmer state of mind. I never forget for long that I could still die from this but it doesn't help to dwell on it too much.

Right now we're at the annual poly party picnic in Meadville. It's called a poly because they used to have a morning party, and evening party, etc., i.e., many parties in one. Now it's just the entire Memorial Day weekend spent camping and drinking beer and picnicking with friends. This is my fifth poly but there have been seventeen so far – always in the same beautiful grove with a creek, old trees, a pavilion, and a lot of flat ground for volleyball and softball.

It's the first time we've seen a lot of people since all our tragedies, and it's wonderful to have everyone's support and love to draw on. Two of our friends, Karen and Roger, have a beautiful little girl who is almost two – she was born the day after our wedding. Roger told us that when they heard about Gwynne's death, they both had the same thought – that we deserved to have Kelly after all we'd been through. That's really touching.

We're enjoying ourselves so much at this poly that we've decided to stay an extra day. Life is so wonderful! Good times, good weather and good friends.

The days just seem to rush by without a break. As long as nothing terminal happens to me, I'm happy that time is going so fast. At this rate, it could all be behind me, just a nasty memory, before I know it!

Tonight the nurses at the HMO learned how to draw blood from my catheter. I commented to the nurse who specializes in oncology (the one that was showing the others how to draw blood) that the chemo wasn't going badly, and that I hadn't gotten sick at all last time. She encouraged me and said, "Just tell yourself you won't get sick next time, too." When she said that I realized I didn't have to tell myself that because I already believe it! I told her, "Oh, I won't. I use hypnosis – it really helps." She didn't look like she believed me, but I believe it. After all, if it's possible for people to be conditioned to throw up when they see their oncologist, it's just as possible to do the opposite.

I've been coughing a little in the mornings and one side of me wants to panic and write my death certificate, while the other side of me says, "Don't be ridiculous! I'm going to have grandchildren!" I want to kill that cancer! I want to have control over it! And hard as I try, I just can't be positive that my mental fight is making a difference (of course, if I'm alive 10 years from now, I'll attribute it to my attitude), I keep thinking about those people who had recurrences in a few weeks and realizing it's possible it could happen to me. Then I turn around and point out to myself that there were twelve people with synovial cell sarcomas that had no recurrence with the chemotherapy, and that <u>will</u> happen to me. It's exhausting to wait to find out if you might be dying – a quick death would be more merciful.

It seems like my hair might be starting to grow back. There are a lot of blonde fuzzy hairs where there used to be dark hair. But it's hard to tell yet if it's going to get longer or just sit there being fuzzy. I hope it grows back! It wouldn't be bad having short hair in the summer and I would certainly feel better! I will that hair to grow! My body is tolerating the drugs while helping to demolish the cancer cells. Kill cancer! Grow hair!

Memorial Day we went to the baby's grave. Her headstone still wasn't there. I called around to get people moving on it – this is ridiculous. I can't help but stare at babies, especially those that seem to be Gwynne's age. The pain is still ever present, and the reminders are all around us. There were even two mailboxes on our street with pink ribbons tied to them signifying the births of girls. Why couldn't they at least have been boys if they had to be born now?

Max tells me that Vicki had her transplant last week and so far is doing really well. She isn't showing any signs of graft versus host disease. Wouldn't it be wonderful if she would end up being fine!

I yelled at Dave tonight for something he probably didn't do (it would be impossible to prove either way).

He got mad and stomped upstairs. It used to be that I would insist I was right and stay angry and we'd be mad for days. Tonight I said to myself, "I could have just as easily been responsible for this. I should apologize," and then I pushed myself up the stairs and apologized (that is so hard for me to do!) Dave was very gracious about it (he knows how hard it is for me) and came downstairs and we shared a pleasant evening. We live together so well!

Anytime I feel like eating meat I just think about how much the lump looked like hamburger and the craving goes away (the comparison is only slightly exaggerated).

At the HMO tonight I saw Dr. Manson, so I guess he'll be taking Dr. Himes's place and Dr. Himes won't stay, after all. Rats!

Tuesday, June 3, 1986

A.D. 25 weeks, 5 days

9:00 p.m.

Friday night it took me 5 hours to get home from work –
we got 3-1/2 inches of rain in one hour just in our
section of town and both the creeks on either side of the
hill we live on flooded. I'm talking flash flood. So far 8
people died in it and 13 are missing. I saw a Blazer being
towed out of the street that was hit the worst. It was
completely smashed and had sticks and mud encrusted
all over it. If someone was in it, they surely died.

Somebody was telling one of my friends that her
grandparents were driving up that street at the time of
the flood and all of a sudden there was this wall of water
coming at them. They couldn't do anything — but
somehow there was air trapped in the car and they got
washed downstream unhurt. Others weren't so lucky.
There was just an incredible amount of water
everywhere. All the roads I tried to take home that night
were covered with water and I kept having to turn
around. And thirty miles away there wasn't even a cloud
in the sky! My grandmother even heard about it on the
news in Holland. This wall of water came roaring over
the bridge I normally cross right at 5:20 p.m. on my way
home from work. It was just weird luck that I was
delayed leaving work and was not on that bridge at my
usual time.

My arm has been sore all weekend. I'm kind of worried about it. I'm kind of worried about everything these days. I had another session with Mom last night but I didn't feel a lot better. I hope I can talk Dr. Stevens into ordering another scan for me. A clear one would make me feel a lot better. An unclear one would make me feel worse, but at least I would know for sure what's going on. The uncertainty is what's so depressing. I'm being hit by a second wave of grief over everything that's happened and that can still happen.

I sent my article in to *Ladies' Home Journal* on Friday. I wonder if they'd buy it?

Wednesday, June 4, 1986

A.D. 25 weeks, 6 days

9:00 p.m.

I feel much better. I went to the doctor today to have my arm checked out and to get chest X-rays. Everything looks good. I could be lucky after all!

Now Dr. Macintyre is leaving the HMO, too! She said that people go to work for an HMO because they want to work less hours and are willing to take less pay. But she's been working 70 hour weeks and then she might as well have a private practice. She's also pregnant. Everybody's pregnant. I wish her the best of luck.

I ran into Dr. Himes. He said he'd been planning to call me before he left. I'm going to miss both of them. But there still is a possibility that I might get to keep Dr. Himes – the HMO's running out of OB/GYN's.

I thanked them both for everything they did for me. They said they hadn't done much – I didn't finish saying it was mostly that they cared that mattered so much.

Saturday, June 7, 1986

A.D. 26 weeks, 2 days

9:30 a.m.

The last couple of days have been rough. I got very sad on Thursday. I couldn't get my mind off the baby. Dave and I both went to the cemetery on our own – we both felt drawn there. The pain just doesn't go away. There are too many other people having babies and talking about them for us to be able to forget what we lost. Last night I dreamed that I was pregnant again and that's what I really want. I'm so jealous of Kathy, who has about six weeks to go. I got invited to her shower next week and it just reminded me of how nice everyone from work was the day I went to the hospital – all the nice baby gifts that are still stacked in the baby's room. I miss her so much. I just ache for her.

Wednesday, June 11, 1986

A.D. 26 weeks, 6 days

Saturday was June's wedding. June lived with my parents for a year when her family abandoned her. She asked Dad to give her away and Mom to light the candle for her, since she considers us more family than her own. It's really sad because the year she lived at our house was pretty stormy and if that was the best year of her life, you have to wonder what the rest of her life must have been like. At any rate her wedding was really nice and I hope her life from now on is happier.

Nicolette was being pursued all evening by one of the ushers (as told by Mom – we didn't go the reception). She finally gave in and fooled around a little with him, "nothing serious". Then she told Danny what she'd done and he got all jealous and possessive and proposed to her! So I hear they set a date for May next year. So soon already!

Also on Saturday Hugo took Angel out. (Angel was his girlfriend for about five years. They broke up a few years ago but apparently couldn't get over each other). Reportedly his intentions were to ask her to marry him but he chickened out and asked her if she'd be willing to move to New York with him. She said she'd think about it! If she'd move for him she'd certainly marry him – wouldn't she? So maybe there will be two weddings next spring! And I intend to be healthily into my second pregnancy by then.

Meanwhile we went to a picnic at Max's house where we saw Dan (of Dan and Vicky) for the first time since the baby died. He seemed well and he said Vicky was being discharged to their temporary apartment in Columbus this week. It looks like she's going to make it! Things are looking good.

I'm actually looking forward to Friday's treatment because it'll be like a Wednesday – over-the-hump-day! I won't have more treatments ahead of me than I've already had Even if they decide to squeeze eight in there, I'll still be half done after Friday. I can't wait! I'm so sick of this catheter (and I just found out that I have to pay for the supplies for it, too!) and I want my hair back.

I am going to have another baby and I am not going to get more cancer because the next baby is going to be born naturally and be breastfed and have a healthy Mom. I don't have room for cancer in my life. (I feel like I do when I'm starting a diet – convincing myself that I have the control to make it happen. I can make myself lose weight – I can make myself not have cancer).

Thursday, June 12, 1986

A.D. 27 weeks

7:15 a.m.

Last night things went downhill fast. I had planned to be home all evening and putter around the house, but at around 6:00 p.m. the nurse from the HMO called to say that the blood they had worked so hard to get out of my catheter on Monday clotted and I'd have to come in to get more blood drawn. That's a half-hour drive plus waiting until they're ready for me. So I went because if I didn't I wouldn't be able to get my treatment on Friday. This time the blood wouldn't come out of the catheter so they finally stuck my arm. At least it only took one stick. This thing isn't worth it. It hurts most of the time, I have to take care of it all the time; I have to sleep with a bra on so I don't pull it out in the middle of the night. I think I'm going to have it taken out after my next treatment.

After my blood was drawn, I talked for a while with the nurse who called me after the baby died and told me that she'd lost one, too. It felt good to talk to someone who knew what it was like but it brought some angry and jealous feelings to the surface. And naturally as I was leaving the building a very pregnant woman came waltzing in, looking mighty unhappy, with her husband running behind her with a bunch of pillows for Lamaze class. I thought the least she could do for me would be to

219

look happy to be pregnant. (Anna Marie, the nurse, told me it really hit her about three months afterwards, too).

So I was thinking about the baby and decided to go to the cemetery and see if her headstone was there yet. When I got there, the headstone wasn't in place, but the foundation had been poured – about four feet below her grave! I thought a headstone belonged at the head of the grave! Or at least at the very foot of it, not four feet away. I'm very upset, to the point of crying. Why does everything have to be so difficult?

12:20 p.m.

All right, so maybe I exaggerated when I said I was looking forward to my next treatment. I'm looking forward to having it over with, anyway. Only a few more hours.

I set the wheels in motion to have the catheter removed. Dr. Stevens said that the ulceration of the skin only happens in 2-3% of the cases. So if it happens to me, I'll play the lottery! Dr. Stevens promised I would not have any more treatments after September 24th, so that's party day! Three more treatments every four weeks, and it'll all be over. Hallelujah! He said my hair probably wouldn't come back until the treatments are over (it is just sitting there being fuzzy). But getting the catheter out at least will be a big relief; I'll be able to go swimming!

One bad effect from all of this is that when I run into people I haven't seen in a long time, I avoid them or even pretend I didn't see them so that I won't have to tell them everything that's happened to me. I could just lie and say I've been fine, thanks, but I don't feel comfortable doing that, either. So I just avoid them.

Maybe in a few months that will go away because I will start to feel that everything is fine.

I called the cemetery yesterday and they said that they put all of the headstones at the foot of the graves in that section. And they don't call them headstones, they call them monuments. No wonder. Maybe they should call them footstones. I wonder if somewhere along the line they told us about this rule of theirs and we were just too distraught to remember it?

Saturday, June 14, 1986

A.D. 27 weeks, 2 days

12:00 p.m.

I got cut off yesterday because the grave salesman from the cemetery called. Someone else can still be buried in the same plot, but they won't put another stone there. So I think we'll buy the plot next to Gwynne's and put one stone for both of us there. He said prices just went up but he's going to try to get us the old price. What pleasant poop this all is!

I told the nurses who give me my treatments that I was going to have my catheter removed and they just jumped down my throat about it. They've seen some of these ulcerations and they said they'd much rather care for a catheter than go through skin grafts. Then they proved just how bad my veins are by comparing my arms to Mom's and one of theirs. Everyone else had veins that popped up even without a tourniquet and mine refused to come up even with one. I guess they're right. The worst is over – why not wait another 84 days?

A.D. 27 weeks, 4 days

9:50 p.m.

This latest treatment was rougher than the previous two. I've been feeling nauseated off and on for the last three days. It's a lot like morning sickness – and if that isn't a thought that strikes terror into my heart. I can think of nothing worse at this time than trying to gauge the damage the drugs might have done and to have to make a decision involving my baby's life again. It just couldn't be possible.

I received a card from Vicky today. It was really up-beat and happy. She's out of the hospital now, living in the apartment with Dan. She mentions how long the summer will be without the baby, but her general tone is incredibly optimistic.

I got a fortune cookie the other day: "What doesn't kill you makes you stronger". Ain't that the truth.

Jan Schoornagel was at my parents' house on Saturday. He's the one that they met when he was treating Dad's best friend, Dolf, at the end of his life. He helped convince me to keep my catheter. He had this way of looking at me that other doctors have, too. It seems like they're trying to figure out if I'm for real or something. Maybe I'm too calm or matter-of-fact for them. Or maybe they just like me and feel sad that I could die from this, or just that I've gone through what I did. It's hard to tell, but it seems to be a universal doctor-look. It makes me a little nervous. It has too much of that appraisal in it, and then I wonder if they're appraising my chances of making it.

I hear so much about nice, decent, honest, good people dying that I really wonder if I'm not meant to be one of those. Just an example to make other people examine their own lives more carefully. But I don't want that! I want to live to retire! I guess the longer I live, the more I'll believe that I'll live long. I want a normal life.

Hugo proposed to Angel on Saturday and she sort of said no. I feel rejected (I'm sure he feels worse). It wasn't a flat-out no, so the saga is still not over.

Wednesday, June 18, 1986

A.D. 27 weeks, 6 days, 10:00 p.m.

The baby's headstone/footstone/monument is finally in place! It's so final – it's really true – we had a baby daughter and she died and she's buried close to where that stone is. It should be right below the stone, but I guess what's done is done. Her actual grave is in the area 3-1/2 – 7-1/2 feet behind the stone.

I spent a long time there, tracing her name with my fingers. The sun was setting and it was incredibly beautiful there. It's a good place to rest. As I was leaving, I saw two deer cavorting in the park. It's an idyllic setting.

We had planned to buy the plot next to Gwynne's because the salesman got us the lower price. I really wanted to do it – I sort of see it as a "family bed". But Dave talked me out of it. He said that's not where our priorities should lie right now. I guess he's right – we don't have the money and it would be better to save for our vacation and our next child. At least when either one of us dies, the other will have insurance money to pay for the funeral.

Saturday, June 21, 1986

A.D. 28 weeks, 2 days

5:40 p.m.

Last night Sue showed us the most haunting picture of her Mom and Dad. Haunting partly because they're both dead now. It was their wedding night and they looked terribly young. He was wearing a black tux and she was wearing a big white dress and besides the car in the picture the rest was completely dark. So his head and she are the only things in the picture that really stand out. I guess it just seems so sad to think that they couldn't know then the fate that awaited them. He died in 1974 just before I met Sue, and her mother died in 1984 two weeks before our wedding. She got hit by a pick-up truck while crossing the street in broad daylight. Life holds no guarantees.

We spent the entire day outside today. It was perfect weather and we mowed and weeded and spruced up the yard and then worked on the deck. It's shaping up into a real beauty. Today was an example of home ownership's hassles and satisfactions.

Sunday, June 22, 1986

A.D. 28 weeks, 3 days

4:00 p.m.

The pain really is going away now. Yesterday was four months since the baby's death and it no longer smarts like an open wound. I can see other children without aching all the time (although sometimes I still do).

Today something strange happened. We were driving along the parkway in the truck with some bookcases in the back for Sue and Rick. All of a sudden I saw us blowing out the right front tire and skidding across the traffic and the truck leaning perilously over on my side. I pulled my arm inside the window and at the same time Dave looked over to me and asked if I had my seat belt on. I said, "Were you thinking about an accident?" and he said yes. When we compared notes, we had both seen exactly the same thing! Freaky, huh?

I keep seeing myself as a lithe athletic beauty with long auburn hair hanging down my back. Considering that I have 20 pounds to go before I re-enter the human race, and then at least 10-15 before I hit lithe, that's quite a vision. Not to mention the long hair. At half an inch a month starting in October sometime, that could take years. But it's a nice vision. I'm not getting this again – once I have my long hair, I'm keeping it.

I haven't been feeling nauseated since the Tuesday after my treatment. Most likely I'm not pregnant (whew!). There's a good time for everything, and after October is a good time for that.

Mom had me "live a dream" during my last session. I dreamt that we were at the beach together, Dave and I, (and I was lithe as ever) and we were snorkeling and pointing out fishes and interesting sights to each other, hand in hand. Then we went back to our rustic beach cottage and conceived our next baby. Then there were scenes of sailing on a catamaran (something I haven't tried yet). Then we were on the plane home, me glowing in the security that I was pregnant. Here I fast forwarded through my pregnancy, went into labor naturally, and in a short time delivered a beautiful baby boy – Ian Kirk Edwards. Next scene: Ian about two, playing on the same beach with us looking on. He had blond curly hair and big blue eyes and sturdy brown legs – a little golden boy. Fade into the sunset.

We're going to make that dream come true.

Tuesday, June 24, 1986

A.D. 28 weeks, 5 days

4:50 p.m.

I was just thinking about the nightmare I had the other night: I was in a house with a bunch of people (friends and family) and we knew there was a tiger in the house (I had read an article on man-eating tigers the evening before I had the nightmare). Against my advice, they decided to turn out the lights so it couldn't see them. I told them that the tiger could see better in the dark than we could, so we were giving it the advantage. They wouldn't listen to me and all took up hiding places in the open living room. I figured that, if I couldn't get the light on, I would at least go in a small room and close the door to keep it out (although I was imaging it breaking down the door to get at me). As I walked into the room I ran smack into the tiger's massive head. I felt more angry than frightened. I yelled at it, "Get out of here!" and at that point. Dave woke me up – I'd been screaming for real.

I just realized that the tiger stalking me was the cancer. I'm in the dark about whether I'm really safe from it, and I'm constantly afraid of running smack into that man-eating beast. I'm frightened of it. But more than that I'm angry at it. But if I try to curl up in bed and wait for it to go away, I may run straight into it – I have to fight aggressively to be able to survive. The subconscious is an amazing thing!

I'm tired of being bald! More hair is growing, but hardly enough to cover my head. If only my hair would come back I'd feel much better. It's not so bad during the day when I wear my wig, but during aerobics class I can't stand to wear it so I just wear a scarf. But I feel very self-conscious – especially with my twenty extra pounds to boot. Soon I'll be thin, svelte and very hairy. Soon.

Friday, June 27, 1986

A.D. 29 weeks, 1 day

7:15 a.m.

My period is late by two days now. That wouldn't be all that unusual except I've had some spotting. That's exactly what happened when I got pregnant with Gwynne. This is just what we need.

9:00 a.m.

It's becoming more and more certain that I'm pregnant. This is the third day in a row of spotting without actually starting my period. If I weren't spotting and my period was just late, I wouldn't be so worried because I would just think the chemo was making me temporarily infertile. But this spotting at the time I should be starting my period is just too much like when I got pregnant with Gwynne. Then I was so worried that I would miscarry from the spotting. Now I keep praying that I start my period or miscarry (since by now I'm convinced I am pregnant).

This is so tough for us. We talked about it for a long time last night. We both feel abortion is wrong for us and yet we're in a position where it's almost the only choice we have. The baby is almost certainly damaged in some way – I had a treatment right after conception. I would have to stop treatments. We would go through nine months of worrying about the baby and me. And when it's born, it could be severely handicapped or brain damaged. And then, if I get a recurrence, we would never be able to say we had given me the best treatment possible. Dave could end up with a damaged child to raise alone.

That's the worst scenario, and then the choice seems clear. But I keep thinking about those first days after conception – the fertilized egg divides on the nutrients from the egg, not the mother's bloodstream. It doesn't implant in the mother's uterus until seven days after conception, and by then the drugs would be out of my body there could be nothing wrong with it. We could be killing our own healthy baby on the chance that it would be damaged.

That seems so inhumane. Even if it were damaged, it seems inhumane to kill it because of that. But then there's my health to consider. What good is it to save a baby at my expense? If I die the baby won't have a mother.

If I really am pregnant, and nature doesn't take care of it (most miscarriages are due to genetic abnormalities – the mother's body rejects an abnormal embryo), we probably will go through with an abortion. But not without a lot of agony on our part. It will not be easy for me. It's not fair for us to have to go through this on top of everything else. As much as we want a baby, why does it have to be now – why not in three months when my treatments are over and we can give the baby everything?

We would talk to some experts first to find out what the damage from the drugs would be. But who is going to assure us that nothing will be wrong with it? In this climate of suits for just about anything, no physician is going to take that chance.

The baby would be due on March 4 -- a month before Gwynne was due. What if the chemo did something to it that makes it able to live inside me but not outside of me? What if we have to go through the same thing again? What if we would have to bury our second child after putting all our energy into making it live? I couldn't take that. But I keep thinking that it must be all right if my body is accepting it. There can't be anything wrong with it. Which is absolutely unreasonable – a lot of babies are born with defects – something could definitely be wrong and it still survive in my womb.

It's not fair! We weren't careless. We use contraceptives every time. What a time for them to fail.

Sunday, June 29, 1986

A.D. 29 weeks, 3 days

7:00 p.m.

Early this morning I was awakened by strong cramps. I started bleeding for a while and then it stopped. Just now I had some more cramping and passed the most incredibly huge clot. Nature is taking care of it! Thank God! It's nice to know, at least, that the chemo is not making me infertile.

Tuesday, July 1, 1986

A.D. 29 weeks, 5 days

11:00 a.m.

Dr. Williams called today just to see how I'm doing! I wasn't home – I was at aerobics class, but Dave talked to him for a while. He remembered all the things I'd been worried about – he asked Dave about all of them. He wanted to know if the chemo was over yet, whether I was getting sick, whether I'd lost my hair. He is such a nice person! Chuck mentioned that Dr. Williams and his wife had been over for dinner, so now I know he does have someone to talk to at home. I wonder if she had to talk him into calling, like, "I'm not sure if I should call – it's just curiosity, it's not my case anymore." – "Sure, honey, call – they'll appreciate knowing that you care." I've been feeling like calling him but I figured he'd be too busy to talk to me. And now he called me out of the blue! I feel pretty special to have the chief of surgery at a major hospital just calling to see how I'm doing!

I talked to Carole today. She told me that her sister-in-law, Marlene, had found out that the baby she was carrying had no head! How horrible! So she had a C-section, because they told her that even if she went to term the baby wouldn't live. No head! How disgusting! That was the kind of choice we almost had to make. Yuk.

Saturday, July 5, 1986

A.D. 30 weeks, 2 days

11:30 p.m.

When we left my parents' house tonight I borrowed the two photo albums that have my baby pictures in them. I wanted to see how much Gwynne and I looked alike as babies. We looked a lot alike.

All the feelings of the past few months washed over me as I looked through the albums. Many of my visions of what Gwynne would be like were based on these pictures that I've looked at all of my life. Each picture in which I see two happy parents protectively hugging their baby girl, I see what should have been us with Gwynne. Oma shouldn't have been here to help bury our daughter, she should have been here to repeat the four generation picture that appears in our photo album.

I guess this lost feeling will never go away. I guess there will always be someone who has a child about the same age. Especially since it seems that the whole world is pregnant or has babies.

I guess all my sad feelings came from having to tell the story to someone from aerobics class that I hadn't seen since I was pregnant. That dreaded question, "I guess you had your baby ...?" No matter how many times I tell the story, no matter how much practice my tongue gets in saying the words, I always get a catch in my throat when I say "the baby died". How could life be so cruel to me?

Dave and I talked for a long time yesterday about having another baby. I said that if it weren't for the chemotherapy, I'd want to get pregnant now. Dave said he wasn't ready yet, that he still had to get over Gwynne. He said he feels like he's run out of reserve emotions and he needs to store up some more before he can go through the anticipation and worry that would come with another baby on the way. He wants to wait a while after the chemo is over – he wants me to be healthy and life to be normal before we go through it again. I understand him from an intellectual viewpoint, but emotionally I want to be carrying another baby as soon as possible. I say it's not to replace Gwynne, but maybe it is. It's like I have this need to have a little body to cuddle and protect and the longer I don't have it, the stronger and more irrational that need becomes. I was so ready to love my baby, and now I don't have an outlet for all that love. Oh God, what I wouldn't give to hold my baby in my arms!

Rationally, we finally concluded to wait three months after the chemo, till around Christmas time, before we start trying for another one. Actually, we don't want to try as much as to just see what happens, but both Dave and I know me well enough to know I'll probably be pretty anxious about it. I know that often interferes with people being able to get pregnant, so I'll try not to be anxious, but it will be difficult.

Monday, July 7, 1986

A.D. 30 weeks, 4 days

10:00 p.m.

Dr. Fisher really upset me today! We were discussing when he would take my catheter out, and he said, "You have to keep in mind that you might have to have more chemotherapy in a year or two, and you might need another catheter then." As if I'm not trying to keep that horrible thought at bay every waking moment! Does he think I don't have to work on my positive attitude? Keeping it in mind would send me over the edge!

I'm sure he thought (or maybe didn't think at all) that my enthusiasm for getting rid of this thing should be tempered by the reality that it might not all be over, not realizing that reality is what I fight day in and day out.

After that I went straight over to Mom and Dad's house and had a hypnosis session to calm me down. I believe that there is no more cancer in my body (Dr. Fisher shook that, but didn't break it). These next three treatments are just a security blanket. My body is concentrating on itself and not allowing anything unusual to grow within it. It can recognize these outlaw cells and get rid of them – and they have been sentenced to death.

240

I will not waste my energy worrying about cancer. I had it once, but I no longer have it and I will not get it back.

I wasn't worried when I went in the hospital to have the lump removed. And it was cancer. I worried for 33 weeks (as soon as I knew I was pregnant) about losing the baby. And I lost her. Worrying did not accomplish a thing – it just made things more difficult. At least not worrying made it easier to go through the surgery.

No, I've learned my lesson. You can think that you can't take something, you can imagine the worst thing that can happen to you, and it just might. It might even get worse than that. But you come through it. You realize all that you have, and it occurs to you that you could lose that, too, and you make up your mind to enjoy everything you have every day and worry about it being taken away from you when it has already happened. At that point you really have something to cry about.

Don't worry about the bullet that didn't hit you.

Besides all that, I'm allowed to go swimming in a regular swimming pool. Not a lake, but a chlorinated pool is okay – as long as my counts are okay.

Wednesday, July 9, 1986

A.D. 30 weeks, 6 days

7:00 am

It occurs to me that for over a year now my life has consisted of count downs. First I was counting down to the end of the summer since I was working in Chicago and wanted to come home. Then I started counting down to the baby's birth. Then I found the cancer and it was a countdown to the end of radiation. Now, of course, I'm counting down to the end of chemotherapy. I'd better stop this – it's no way to live.

I looked at my blood counts yesterday. They were low, except for platelets. I wonder how I can feel so good if my counts are low? I can't help it – I can't wait till this is all over.

4:00 a.m.

My treatment yesterday was the worst since my first one. I got up twice at night to empty my stomach. We were just discussing why it might have happened. I guess it was due to eating lunch and dinner – drawing more blood to my stomach and thus creating more irritation. All I know is that I ate dinner after my treatment the first time, and I skipped it the next three times, and now when I had a little dinner I threw up again. Plus, I had a relatively heavy and late lunch. Oh well, something new to tell the doctor.

Mom was telling me a while ago that she once asked Dave if he thought about what it would be like now if the baby were alive and he said, "All the time!" with such emphasis that it struck her heart. He doesn't show it, but he's suffering a lot. I hope the near future brings us some relief from our suffering. Only two more treatments to go! August 8th and September 5th. Then I can get my catheter out (hopefully September 8th). Less than 8 weeks to go! Hallelujah! And my hair is getting more plentiful if not less fuzzy. The nurses said it was conceivable that I might have a full head of hair before the end of treatments. I've started washing what I have with shampoo again (I was just soaping my head since we shaved it). Just a drop of shampoo does the trick – it makes me happier.

Dr. Johnson told me that he had no idea what Dr. Fisher was talking about. I'm not getting any more treatments unless I have a recurrence. Thank God for that! I told him I intended to live my life normally, as if there were no threat of cancer, and he seemed to appreciate my attitude.

Friday, July 18, 1986

A.D. 32 weeks, 1 day

4:00 a.m.

There are so many things whirling through my head that I can't sleep. I'm really upset that I got passed over for promotion once again. Looking at it from my boss's perspective, I can see why – I guess it's not a promotable feature to continue to do your job well even under all the pressure I've been under. Admirable, maybe, but not promotable. I feel so <u>frustrated</u> because I know I was given less work on the project because I was pregnant (I know because Terri told me so). And that made sense because I was due in the middle of the project, and it's really hard to replace someone that's doing the "promotable" stuff in the middle of the project. It would certainly be worth it if the baby had lived, but it's so frustrating to have such a setback in my career and to have lost the reason I was willing to take it. Damn, my luck is just incredible. And even now, I can't really be available for work in the field because I have to be around home for doctor's appointments, so the cancer has a hand in keeping me down, too.

I'm frustrated all around, too. The work I have to do now is boring, I don't have enough time to do everything I want to do; I don't have enough money to do what I want to do. My weight loss is so slow that it might as well be non-existent; I feel like a real porker. It would be really nice to have some good luck for a change – and I don't count not getting caught in the flash flood on June 3rd as good luck (simply because I could have been caught in it, and wasn't, isn't exactly good luck).

It's not fair! I never get told that I do a bad job. I just need more experience of the right kind to be promoted and my life keeps interfering with my ability to get it.

Well. I had decided a few months ago that this is not a good time to get worked up over my career, and if I just keep doing my job well, my time will come. I guess now that I've got it all out, I can return to that philosophy – it's just hard to watch other people get promoted around you. I guess I have to keep on truckin'.

Sunday, July 20, 1986

A.D. 32 weeks, 3 days

Many times as I catch a glimpse of my bald head (now fuzzy) in the mirror, I'm transported back to that morning in the shower when I found the lump. The panic, the fear, the relief when I found out I had a 99.9% chance of it being benign. And then that phone call. The phone call that changed my life irreparably. There are times when I'm so overwhelmed by it all that I wish I could escape back to my past, live it over again with a different outcome. Why does it have to be this way? Why must everything be so difficult? I have to struggle to stay on top of it all and it's so easy to topple me. I have it easy compared to some, but living with cancer is never easy.

I want to know that I'm going to be all right and that the anguish will stop. I want some guarantees, and there are none.

Tomorrow the baby would have been five months old. The raw pain is gone, but every child I see calls up a dull ache.

Tuesday, July 22, 1986

A.D. 32 weeks, 5 days

10:00 p.m.

My cousin Aline is visiting my parents from Holland. She's 13 (exactly half my age). I was sitting in my parents' living room looking at her and thinking back to when I was thirteen, visiting her parents and holding her in my lap at four months of age. It suddenly made me very angry to realize that if things had gone right, she would be holding my baby now. It's so unfair, dammit! It also happened to be the day Gwynne would have been five months old. Life sucks sometimes.

Sunday, July 27, 1986

A.D. 33 weeks, 3 days

10:00 p.m.

People who work in the "healing professions" can be terribly insensitive. First Dr. Fisher made his comment about me needing more chemotherapy, and then Dr. Johnson's nurse made the same comment when I said I was going to have the catheter removed. Then when I explained what a giant pain in the neck it was, she said, just like Dr. Fisher, "I guess you could always have another one put in." What do these people expect? That I keep this stupid thing in for five years until my chances of recurrence are minimal? Everyone says a positive attitude is half the battle – I wouldn't consider that a positive attitude. Besides, why live with a foreign object coming out of your body unless it was a necessity (as it appears to be now)? Why don't they say, "You probably won't need chemo again, so take it out and treat a recurrence if it comes about"? At least Johnson and Stevens talk like that, and they're the ones that count.

7:30 a.m.

The last couple of days I would stop in the middle of something and imagine what Gwynne would be like if she were alive today. Every time I think I'm over it I have a few bad days and realize how hard this has been on me.

Now that I'm through it and looking back, I can't believe that I withstood all the pressure I was under when I was pregnant, working and going to radiation treatments every day. I'm glad I had Mom's hypnosis to pull me through it. But what really got me through it was hope for the baby, and the joyful thought of her arrival.

Less than six weeks to go. I'm getting impatient. And I'm not going to let this come back and ruin my life again.

Saturday, August 2, 1986

A.D. 34 weeks, 2 days

10:00 a.m.

I've been feeling very angry. Kathy's baby is due any day now and several other people I know are pregnant. Why couldn't I go through my pregnancy without problems and end up with my baby? So many people have babies who won't treat them as well as we would treat ours, and it's so unusual for a baby to die, why did it have to happen to us? I don't understand why we have to go through all of this!

I'm getting sick and tired of this cancer. I have a treatment on Friday and I'm just too tired to go through it. My muscles have been sore; my joints have been aching – I'm really starting to feel like I'm sick. (The phrase "sick and tired" really has meaning here). I guess I couldn't expect my body to keep on behaving normally when it's being poisoned.

The pain in my side that I've been worried about is probably a small hernia in my diaphragm. At least that's what I saw under hypnosis last night. I looked at my diaphragm and saw a small tear in it and some tissue poking through it. I was amazed! Even in trance I kept thinking, "It's a hernia! I know what it is!" It's a plausible explanation for the pain, too. What's interesting about it is that it started to hurt when I had to review another employee in the company, who hadn't done a very good job when he worked for me but who thought very highly of himself, so the bad review wasn't what he expected. I knew he wouldn't accept responsibility for his own actions, and I was right – he's been angry with me ever since. He's been a thorn in my side, so to speak. This is another time when a folk saying becomes appropriate.

This pain is forcing me to slow down and take it easier on my body, and I believe that's what's needed right now. It makes sense for my body to create a signal to slow down when I wasn't doing it on my own.

I'm becoming more and more convinced that your mental state affects your physical state and vice versa.

I don't know when the cancer started growing, but it had to be sometime last summer. At least that's when my arm hurt the most. Last summer I was living in Indiana with Terri while we did a project that I didn't particularly enjoy, and only coming home every other weekend. Then I got pregnant and realized that I couldn't make a choice between motherhood and career and I couldn't do both well. I'd have to give up advancing in my career for the baby, and I wouldn't be able to be a full-time mother for her. At the time I couldn't see anything positive in it, and it was eating away at me. (Obviously, another folk saying that makes sense). Getting cancer at that time forced me to re-evaluate my life and priorities, and could have allowed me to just rest, quit working and take it easy, if I had wanted to do that. I'm glad I didn't, but next time things will be different: I'll have enough money in the bank to be able to stay out on maternity leave for more than four weeks, and I'll remember that I can always advance in my career after my children are older. Many people have switched careers in their 30s or 40s and done well enough; there's no rush for me to get ahead now when what I really want is a family.

I only wish I had some guarantees that this whole scenario wouldn't repeat itself. I couldn't stand losing another baby.

Sunday, August 3, 1986

A.D. 34 weeks, 3 days

1:30 p.m.

Kathy just called to tell me she had her baby last night. Brian Michael, 7lbs. 5oz. My guess was off by 8oz – I thought he would be bigger (I knew it was a boy, though). I had a feeling yesterday that that was the day. I told Dave about it and he said, "Everyone else gets to have babies ... I'm selfish aren't I?" I don't think he's any more selfish than anyone else – we both feel cheated, especially when someone else has a healthy one. Kathy and I have been sharing experiences up to now – at this point I don't have any more advice for her. It feels awfully lonely.

This morning I was thinking that I'd just about had enough of the chemotherapy, since it's finally catching up to my body and affecting my overall health and at that moment, just to prove my point I guess, my syringe slipped and I tried to catch it and it stuck into my middle finger all the way to the bone! It's a big bruise now. It didn't hurt that much but it was a big shock – I'd been so used to handling those things that I was getting careless. Dave completed the routine of injecting Heparin into my catheter while I held ice on my finger and talked him through it. He's so good to have around! He'd be such a good Daddy. Well, maybe as soon as December we can get started on another one. No matter how many

254

precautions I get from well-meaning health professionals, I am cured and I am not going to need any more treatment. I may even cancel the last chemo treatment – except I'd rather follow the doctors' plans to keep them happy. I don't have any more cancer though, so the chemo really isn't necessary anymore.

I went to see Kathy and her baby. I was okay until I came back home, and then I felt really blue. It's so hard.

Then I went with Dave to Barb and Rick's house just to keep from staying home alone. Dave is painting their addition, and I usually come along with him so I can visit with Barb, but we didn't expect them to be home today. When we got there, they had just come home, so I went in to talk to Barb for a while. I told her how I was feeling and then she told me about Rick's friend, Allan. Allan and his wife had a six-year-old, a two-year-old, and a brand new baby. A few days ago, everyone was playing with the new baby and the two-year-old wandered off and fell into the pool and drowned. Rick went to the funeral and Barb said she couldn't stop thinking about us. I offered to talk to Allan and his wife if they needed to talk, but I'm sure they won't feel comfortable with that. I can certainly imagine how they feel – especially the guilt over not having prevented an accident like that from happening in the first place.

I suggested to Barb that she make sure that she and Rick were always available to listen and talk about the child that died, because time may heal but it does not take the child out of your everyday thoughts.

Today I read over the events surrounding Gwynne's death and I cried, but there are many more times that I think about her, maybe fleetingly, but she's still a part of my life. Like the other day, I saw a couple in a school yard teaching their son how to ride a bike, and I thought to myself, "Five years from now I won't be able to teach my daughter how to ride a bike." I bet those kinds of thoughts never really go away.

Barb told me that I could always talk to her about Gwynne when I want to. She wanted to make sure I knew that. She's a good friend.

Wednesday, August 6, 1986

A.D. 34 weeks, 6 days

So much for my theory about a hernia in my diaphragm – the nurses told me that my pain is in the wrong place for that. It's probably a muscle. What did I see in trance then? Something similar, or did I just make it up? This is something to ask Mom about.

8:30 p.m.

A lot has been going on in the last few days. Tuesday I went to Barb's house along with Leslee and Mary Ellen for pizza and to watch Dr. Ruth Westheimer's tape on better sex. Naturally we hardly listened to a word of it and spent most of the time talking to each other. It was a meeting of "the four musketeers" (as we called ourselves when we always ate lunch together when we worked together). When the conversation turned serious, we started talking about trying to control your life. I started to say that I thought I might have allowed the cancer to start because I was trying to control too much of my life and that I was slowly learning to relinquish that control and just let things happen, but it had taken a major crisis to teach me that. Both Barb and Mary Ellen have had to deal with difficult situations, and suddenly we all found ourselves saying we were at peace with ourselves, finally. And we were not worrying about the situations we couldn't control. Maybe that's something that happens when you get to your mid-twenties. But I think many people never experience that. Mary Ellen calls it "putting it in God's hands" and I guess I do, too, given my perception of God.

Then yesterday I went to a writers' meeting so I could figure out how to turn this journal into a book to show people it's still possible to be happy after a tragedy (or two). I was nervous because I didn't know what to expect. My first surprise was that I knew the person whose house we were in (from church). And there were two other people from church as well. After the meeting started, I felt even better, because I realized that these people were very supportive and were collectively helping each other improve their work. Plus, it was very interesting to hear stories people make up and have input into changes they make. It reminded me of my poetry class in college, which I enjoyed more than any other class and which made my poetry mature by leaps and bounds.

There was a tense moment (on my part) when Linda asked why I had wanted to come. It was hard to talk to a room full of people about what I've been through, but all I had to do was say that I wanted to publish the journal I started on the day I found out I had cancer, and after a brief moment of somewhat stunned silence, everyone started giving helpful suggestions. Now I feel comfortable with the thought of bringing copies for people to read – I think I'll start with the article I sent to *Ladies' Home Journal* and go from there. I also think I'll keep going to these meetings – I really enjoyed it and it's so different from any other things I do. It's almost like being back in school!

In all the excitement, I almost forgot that I saw Dr. Johnson yesterday as well. I've lost over 10 lbs. since I started chemo! (Not from chemo, from eating better and less). Dr. Johnson wants me to have another scan before taking the catheter out, but he said I could have the scan before the last treatment so I can have the catheter taken out right after the Sept. 5th treatment (Sept. 8th, then) – if the scan is clear. He said he expected it to be clear – so do I. He said the pain in my side is most likely from an intercostal muscle and I should just take it easy. The tired muscles that I felt in aerobics are a cumulative effect from the chemo and will go away after the treatments but probably get worse until then. He's going to give me more Ativan (an anti-nausea drug) this treatment. He said it's unusual to get sick after you've had so many uneventful treatments.

After the chemo is over and I've had a clear lung scan, I'll just be coming back periodically for checkups. He strongly suggested that we wait about six months before starting another baby to make sure any residual effects from the chemo have worn off. That seems like a tolerable amount of time. He also said that it's not unusual to gain a few pounds after a treatment (which happens to me regularly) and I shouldn't worry about it. I'm starting to like him a lot better.

I'm jealous of Leslee. She somehow has the energy to get up every morning at 5:45 a.m. and run/walk 3-1/2 miles. Seven days a week she does this, and she's lost 10 lbs. and eats everything in sight. I wish I could do that. But I just can't stand to get up so early and my muscles are so tired. Maybe after the chemo is over. Or maybe I could just get myself used to one mile at a time. Oh God! So much to do, so little time!

My hair is covering my head now! A few more weeks and off goes the wig!

6:00 p.m.

Thursday I walked/ran two miles and then I had a treatment on Friday. I slept all night and got up at 6:30 a.m. to puke. I just put it off longer, that's all. But after I threw up a second time I felt much better than usual. We went to the summer picnic held by my company and had a decent time. Kathy was there with Brian, not even a full week old yet. I got to hold him and goo and ga over him. I can't believe Gwynne was almost two pounds smaller than that – babies are such miracles.

Aline went back to Holland today. It's too bad – I hardly got to see her and she's such a good kid. It's been raining and blah all day. I haven't really gotten out of bed yet and I don't really feel like it.

I went to the picnic without my wig. Since everyone from work has seen me that way, off it stays!

Tomorrow is our second wedding anniversary. We've only suffered through living separately (while I was working in Chicago), cancer, and the death of our child in two years. I wonder what excitement lies ahead of us? Sometimes I think about "taking responsibility" for your own life – the trend these days is to sue anyone you can when something goes wrong in your life – I could certainly find enough reasons to sue someone. But the underlying belief must then be that <u>someone else</u> is to blame for your troubles, no matter what they are. When I bring up the possibility of having allowed the cancer to grow at a certain time in my life, maybe to bring about a crisis that would eventually better my life, I invariably encounter resistance. People don't want me to take responsibility for what's happening in my own body. I'm not sure I want to, myself, but the alternative is even more frightening – could my body be allowing more killer cells to live against my will? Better to blame myself for the past, forgive myself, and go on to forge a more peaceful future. But this idea frightens many people. If I'm to blame for my own cancer, possibly they're responsible for their problems, too.

Tuesday, August 12, 1986

A.D. 35 weeks, 5 days

6:00 p.m.

I wish I could say our second anniversary was fantastic, but we both had too much on our minds to be truly happy. I kept thinking about our last anniversary – we were expecting our first baby, we had enough money in the bank to go house hunting, and we were healthy. It made me miss the baby so much!

We went out to dinner and Dave told me how it hurt him to hold Kathy's baby at the picnic – how he didn't get enough of holding Gwynne. He told me that at the times he feels the most pain, no one can help him through it; he just has to suffer it until it's over, and then he's happy to have people to turn to. He says he's been pushing his grief away and sometimes he tries to force it out but it's always out of reach. He's always watching the way other men treat their children, and then he'll make a comment to me like, "Tom doesn't hold his new baby much ..." and I can fill in the rest, "not as much as I would have held Gwynne." It's so sad.

Then, in turn, I was talking about how frightened I was. Mondays after a treatment are always bad because the nausea hasn't gone away and I feel really vulnerable. But yesterday was especially bad because they called me to schedule my next scan. It's a week from today, and everything hinges on it being clear.

Friday, August 15, 1986

A.D. 36 weeks, 1 day

9:30 p.m.

When I was about 4-1/2 months pregnant, I was doing exercises in aerobics class and noticed that my arm, which was hurting, looked funny. "So that's it," I thought, "it's out of joint and that's why it hurts!" For months now I've been wondering why I never bothered to look at my arm again or tried to make it "go out of joint" again. You would think that would be the first thing I would do – I've never had a sprained ankle without constantly checking how bad the swelling was, for instance.

I also remember a few weeks later driving home from work and passing the cemetery where Dee is buried (Mom's friend who died at 44 of a cerebral hemorrhage). I passed it every day, but that night it was dark and my arm hurt every time I shifted gears, and I couldn't get my mind off dying and how sad it would be if I died suddenly. I imagined people at my funeral and actually started crying!

I realized today, in a flash of insight, what was going on then. I knew what I had. I knew it was deadly. But I didn't want to know – at least not until my pregnancy was far enough along to be able to save the baby. If I had "discovered" the lump then, everyone would have

266

pressured me to have an abortion – it would have been too long to wait for treatment. And I did not want to even have to consider killing my baby for my own sake. So I simply "discovered" the lump when the baby had a chance. And it almost worked, too – without that infection, Gwynne was a big, healthy baby.

That explains why I refused to acknowledge it, but not how it was able to start. Did it start before I got pregnant? I think so; I remember my arm hurting most of the summer, and I didn't know I was pregnant until the end of July. I was very unhappy then, but making the best of it. I didn't want to leave Dave for my career and yet I thought I had to sacrifice for it. We'd only been married eight months when I left for Chicago. And on our first anniversary I had to take a vacation day to be able to stay home for it. Could the cancer have been a way to show me what my priorities really are? Could it have started when I spent every day hating what I was doing and wishing I was home with Dave? I suppose I could consider it a benefit from the disease that no one can consider sending me out of town for a long time; if not out of sympathy, then out of necessity because I have so many doctors' appointments. Then getting pregnant didn't help because it threw me into a tizzy over my career and how I was going to manage everything. I was certainly under enough stress to invite my body to rebel.

Enough introspection already! We had some great news yesterday: The old cabin property we've been trying to sell is sold – for $9,000! I'm really happy about it – we had been negotiating with the neighbor who "only wanted it to keep someone else from building on it." We were prepared to settle for $6,500, but he didn't go over $5,000. In the meantime, someone called Dave's parents and asked them if it was true that they were selling it and asking $8-11,000 for it. Then he said he was interested in it because he wanted to build a house and he really liked the site! Two days and some quick negotiations later, he thought he had a good deal, we thought we got a good price, and I'm happy because it's going to someone who appreciates it and not the surly neighbor! We've already had our first argument over what to do with the money (besides saving at least 1/3 of it). Dave wants new tools and I want to put in a bathroom upstairs so we can move our bedroom up there and be close to our next little baby.

I'm feeling a mixture of anxiety and elation over the scan on Tuesday. At the beginning of the week I was afraid to feel elated, but by now I can't help myself! It will all be over September 5th! My treatment will be early in the morning and my catheter will be out by the afternoon! I'm so excited! And with the extra money, we can afford to take that vacation without worrying. I kept thinking I didn't really want to go, with our bank account so low, but after hearing about the sale I realized how much I wanted to go!

I have to go out of town August 21-29. I'm going to D.C. for some training, but every time I think about it I get anxious. (Harking back to Chicago, maybe?) If there's anything wrong with the scan, I'm simply not going. But one week is not four months and I'll be okay.

In three weeks it will all be over (we hope and pray and rant and rave)! I think Vicky's coming home Sept. 6th – what a coincidence! Mom was telling me yesterday how insensitive people can be about the baby's loss. She thought people didn't expect grandparents or even fathers to be as hard hit as the mother (she started crying as she was talking about it – it's obvious that it still bothers her a lot, too). She talked about one man at her office whose daughter had a baby a few months before I did – a girl – and how he was excitedly showing her pictures of the baby, never realizing that she might be upset to think about the granddaughter she didn't have anymore. She even bought overalls the other day – she found herself walking to the checkout with them before she realized the baby she was buying them for was dead. I told her she should force the issue – that's what I do. I told her to look at those pictures and say, "Your granddaughter is beautiful – she makes me think of my granddaughter." If people are being insensitive, educate them (gently if possible) on how long and halting the grieving process is. Not only that, but let out those feelings. Saying that you miss someone sometimes helps – talking about how you feel and having other people acknowledge your feelings makes them easier to accept. I love talking about the baby, my pregnancy and her birth. I'm not going to let people deny me the experience of motherhood because they don't know what to say – I'd rather tell them exactly how I feel. And, usually, they get more comfortable with it (especially if they really care) and they even start asking questions. When someone is so interested in me that she's asking questions about how I feel, isn't that the ultimate in communicating? How could I take that any way but positively? I wish I could shake people out of being polite and just get them to be open.

Tuesday, August 19, 1986

A.D. 36 weeks, 5 days

5:20 p.m.

Well, the CAT scan is over. Now all we have to do is wait for the results. This time it went very smoothly. I didn't even have to talk them into using the catheter. I'm afraid to hope.

Saturday I want to the drug store to pick up my Heparin and I found out that I couldn't buy a small quantity – it had to be 25 bottles (50 days' worth). So the pharmacist said, "If I were you. I'd keep it in a cool dark place. That way it'll stay good – you'll probably need it again in the future anyway." This time I got annoyed. I looked him straight in the eye and said, "Don't say that! I'm not going to need it anymore!" He said, "Oh yes, we hope that's true ..." Why don't they all just start digging my grave?

I also bought running shoes on Saturday. I walked/jogged one and a half miles Saturday, one on Sunday, and two yesterday. Today I'm still lethargic from the Benadryl I had to take to keep from getting the reaction to the contrast.

11:45 p.m.

Dave told me today how he used to feel indifferent towards babies. He thought they were kind of funny-looking. But now every time he sees a baby, especially a really little one, he feels a sad longing. He pays so much attention to our friends' children and their interactions with the world. Someday he'll be a better Daddy because of what we've been through. Kathy brought her baby in to work today and I held him and fed him and even got him to burp. I suddenly felt impatient and gave him back to Kathy. I went back to work but all day long I kept smelling that special baby smell on my clothes. Thinking about it just now made me burst into tears. The way his little head just nestled against my cheek was too much for me to bear.

I went to the writers' club today and I brought my article and the first three entries of the journal. There wasn't a dry eye in the room and no one had any criticism except that they wanted some things clarified. It was extremely encouraging!

Now if only my scan will come back positive, I can end this nightmare already.

Saturday night after Chinese dinner at a new place, I got terrible stomach cramps. It got so bad that I considered going to the hospital. At that point I woke Dave up. I asked him to get my first aid stuff out of the car, and after I took my pulse and blood pressure, I became satisfied that it wasn't internal bleeding like Sue had. I had to look something up in my first aid book, and I came upon a picture of the human anatomy. The diaphragm appears on the picture just where my pain has been. Maybe I was right after all!

One thing is for sure! If I have to sit and type this whole book, I'm going to have to invest in a new chair. My aching back!

I found out Kathy was at work today to resign so she can stay home with her baby. I don't blame her, but I'll miss her.

Thursday, August 21, 1986

A.D. 37 weeks

10:00 p.m.

The scan was clear, the scan was clear, THE SCAN WAS CLEAR! It's all going to be over in 14-1/2 days!!! I'm on cloud nine! Could it be true? Could my future hold good health and a family? I'm starting to dare to hope that September 5th will be the last discomfort I'll have to suffer from this cancer. I'm going to live! Hallelujah! I'd better keep taking care of myself. I'm not going to let this happen again.

How ironic that my last treatment, my independence day, should fall almost exactly nine months from the day my cancer was diagnosed. My new life was conceived then ... September fifth I'll be reborn! A new life, a new beginning. I get a second chance!

I've been so on edge that I couldn't sleep. Now my lids are drooping. I can finally rest a little easier.

1:30 p.m.

I feel so happy! I just combed my hair! How long has it been? Five months? Not only that, but it's definitely showing some wave. It used to be wavy – I'm hoping for curly now. After my last treatment (in 13 days!) I'm going to treat myself to a trip to the hairdresser – for a "trim". It won't be much of one, but it's one step closer to normalcy. After that one, I'm going to need more of them! Imagine getting excited about needing a haircut!

It feels like the good old days. Dave is playing music loudly in the living room and I feel great! It's going to be hard not to worry about a recurrence once I stop going to treatments, but at least life is getting easier all the time. Maybe next year we'll be expecting another baby at this time!

Tomorrow I'm leaving for Washington, D.C. until Friday. But time is going so fast, it will be gone in a wink and then it'll be only one week until freedom!

Hm. It looks like the sale of the property fell through because the buyer couldn't get the money. It was too good to be true anyway. But we don't need extra money to be happy! We've got each other. (Except I just broke the mower so maybe we do need extra money to pay for that.)

I wanted to get the lawn mown before leaving since Dave is working once again. I feel bad about breaking the mower, but I can't do anything about getting it fixed since it's Sunday.

I went to the cemetery today. I found out that if I sit with my back against the back of the "monument" (footstone), my feet touch the bottom of her grave. It's good to know, because the grave's distinction will be gone by Spring.

I drove by the old part of the cemetery and found some other people who loved and lost their children:

Eva C. Carr, wife of Wm. C. Edwards

1896-1923

At the bottom of this monument there was:

Evelyn E. Edwards

1923-1929

Did Evelyn's mother die in childbirth? And then poor Evelyn didn't live too long herself. How did Wm. C. feel about it all? I bet he was a pretty sad guy. Eva was 27 when she died.

Then there were Annie C. and Elizabeth H. Ringlehaltz. Annie was born in 1891 and died in 1892. Elizabeth was born in 1897 and died in 1899. Their parents were buried next to them: Henry, 1862-1935 and Susanna, 1873-1952. Susanna was 18 when Annie was born, and 24 when Elizabeth was born. I wonder if they had more kids? They must have. Annie and Elizabeth's little markers said "daughter" like Gwynne's: we want people who see our children's graves to know they had parents who loved them.

Monday, August 25, 1986

A.D. 37 weeks, 4 days

5:15 p.m.

It all started with the bullet-proof glass. We thought it must just be Washington, D.C., but it turned out it was the hotel. After clumping up the metal staircase outside, we got to the balcony to find our rooms right next to the stairs. I got into my room, went to the bathroom, and heard Tracy's door go "boom"! Ten seconds later she was knocking on my door, "I have to change rooms. My phone and radio have been pulled out of the wall." I said to her that she could stay in my room since I'd rather have someone else in the room when anyone could walk past it. As I said it, to the tune of someone clunk, clunking up the stairs, I sat down on the bed, which said, "pthhh!" (like a fart). Every time I moved, the bed said "pthhh" again. We looked at each other, grabbed our bags, and checked out. We laughed hysterically all the way to the hotel we're in now, which has noiseless beds, insulated halls, and intact phones. I assume the noisy bed was to make unmarried people feel guilty for having sex on it, but that's just an assumption.

I'm having a great time traveling with Tracy. She's good company. Totally honest (so I feel free to be, too) and she has the same preferences I do (such as reading over an evening at the bars). This week isn't going to be so bad after all.

278

10:00 p.m.

I was thinking about holding my dead baby in my arms (at dinner Tracy and I talked about her death at length). I didn't know anything about how or what she might have felt. Her life before her birth was a mystery to me. (And to her?) I knew enough about it that it intrigued me, but it was always a mystery.

Her death couldn't have been any more of a mystery to her than her birth must have been – and it probably was more comfortable than her life was. She struggled so hard to live; Dave's description of her tiny chest heaving is proof of that. But her death couldn't have been violent or unhappy. Her face looked at peace. I instantly knew she wasn't mine any more. I wonder now why I didn't kiss her or cradle her head in my hand – I wanted to do that but it wasn't right. It's only something I wanted to do if she was alive. I didn't examine her or even take off her bonnet (which is why I didn't want to cradle her head). I didn't lift up her shirt either. I touched her arms and legs, fingers, toes, tiny nails, but I never kissed her or cradled her. Because she wasn't alive. She was beautiful, soft, warm. purple, but not alive. And if I doubted it, the fluid dripping from her nostril proved it.

But if dying is something my innocent, beautiful baby did, it can't be terrible. It is natural, and inescapable. It frightens those of us who are afraid of the unknown, but we got through birth okay – death must just be another transition.

I'm not afraid of it. I'm afraid of missing people who die, but that is also part of life. It doesn't make me any more likely to die than someone who fears it; I can live a long full life without feeling that I'm holding my death at bay.

One thing I would never want is to be kept alive by "heroic" means. Death is not the enemy, to be staved off at any cost. It's the natural termination to life as we know it, perhaps a new beginning to a different life. If I'm incapable of continuing my life on my own, is it fair to trap me in my body just to ward off death?

Death, like cancer, is a word that frightens people. I've been advised to strike the word "cancer" from my vocabulary, maybe "death" should have the same fate. But what does that accomplish? I <u>had</u> cancer, someday I <u>will</u> die. Whether the two will be related, only time will tell, but it doesn't really matter. I'm not afraid of my cancer either. It's not <u>the</u> cancer, or <u>a</u> tumor, it's <u>my</u> cancer. I accept it as a part of my life, but it is not bigger than my life. I live around it for now, I'll live with a memory of it for the rest of my life. It may be the end of a chapter, but it's not the entire book by any means.

Tuesday, August 26, 1986

A.D. 37 weeks, 5 days

8:00 a.m.

I just saw a report on a 9-year-old named Jenny who got 3rd place in a karate tournament – right after surgery for a brain tumor. Way to go, Jenny! She wants to become a black belt karate instructor. Her doctors are hoping for a complete recovery – so am I. What a kid!

Later

Those cereal commercials are really getting on my nerves. They start out with a sincere-looking yuppie type saying something like, "I'm only 26 *(31, 33, whatever)*. I'm too young to worry about cancer." *Wrongo, bucko.* "So, when the NCI recommended a higher fiber diet to prevent certain kinds of cancer," *(not too many; cancer of the intestinal tract mostly)* "I didn't pay too much attention. Then I started thinking, if I can make changes now, such as eating cereal with high fiber, and get great taste in the bargain, isn't that a good start?" *Yeah, right. Cereal can prevent cancer. Give me a break. Changing your lifestyle might, if you have a bad lifestyle, but cereal?* I want to strangle that stupid man with my bare hands!

Tuesday, September 2, 1986

A.D. 38 weeks, 5 days

9:45 p.m.

Wow, has life been busy! I got back from Washington to find that Dad had sold my car for me! That's just great, except I didn't really expect it, so I had to go running out to find a new car. I found a nice one that I really like, and I got a good deal on it, and Thursday we're going down to the dealer to trade cars, so it's all working out well. The new car did really well in the crash tests, so our next baby will be safe when it's in the car.

Then I spent the rest of Saturday running errands (picking up my new desk chair) and finding Dad a birthday present. We went out to our favorite restaurant again and our favorite waiter, Pete, was so happy to see us that he brought us two glasses of champagne (even though he wasn't even waiting on us that night). From there we went to Mom and Dad's house to give Dad his presents. Dad liked them. Then Dad and Dave watched the football game while Mom and I made apple pie (the Dutch way, which is not the same as Dutch apple pie, believe it or not). It was a pleasant fall (or almost fall) evening.

Sunday we went to Harrisburg for Pete and Jill's anniversary party. We saw some of the people from the Poly party there, which is nice. Karen and Roger and

Kelly were there; Kelly is still as cute as ever. They're planning another trip to the beach next summer, with about 12 people – so far. We told them we were definitely up for going next summer (as long as I'm healthy – which I should be)!

We spent most of Monday driving home. We missed the exit for the Turnpike, so we ended up taking a smaller highway through some really quaint towns. It was worth the extra time on the road for the scenery. Would that trip be beautiful in October, with the leaves all turning!

We spent the evening doing a few odds and ends around the house – replacing the lock on the kitchen door and the doorknobs on the closets. Putzing, American style!

When we arrived home, the cats were waiting for us on the back deck (still unfinished – maybe it can still be done before winter, if Dave's jobs slow down a little). We left them and their food outside since they seem to be happier outside. Apparently Cookie had been meowing all night to get in, because she could barely squeak when we got home! We kept trying to make her meow to hear that sound again, but she would have none of it. She was pretty mad at us, even though she had stayed out all night Friday night and had us all worried. I guess we're not supposed to do that to her (kitty double standards).

The next few days are still chock full of activities. Today I cleaned out my car but didn't get a chance to vacuum it. I probably won't either – tomorrow morning I have to see Dr. Johnson, then I have to work late to make up for it, and then I have to go to the writer's meeting at 7:00 p.m. Thursday I trade cars, and then Friday morning I have my treatment and get the catheter out! Busy, busy, busy. I'll probably be more excited Saturday, when I have a new car and no catheter to enjoy. Right now all I can think about is the treatment and more surgery. Yuk. But, it's almost over!

11:30 p.m.

It's late, but I have a lot to write about.

My visit to Dr. Johnson was quick and uneventful. He wants me to come back in two months and he doesn't need any more blood draws from me. I'll be free! From now on, I'll just have periodic check-ups, chest X-rays, and blood chemistries done. But most of the time, I'll be a regular person! He said that I should wait six months before I get pregnant, but when I said, "How about three months?" he replied that the time limit was based on theory; there is no real proof of danger after the end of chemotherapy.

This evening I went to the writers' group, where I got involved in two very interesting discussions. The first discussion was an aside with Pat, who appears to have the most experience of the group with writing in "the real world". We were talking about how people seem to time illnesses so that they are not necessarily awful: Pat caught the same flu as her husband but it got worse and worse until she ended up in the hospital. While she was sick, she caught herself thinking, "What a relief, I don't have to go to work," when her job was really tense and high pressure. Then when the illness became painful, she decided, "Well, this isn't any fun either," and she was amazed at how fast she recovered.

After I related my opinions, we started talking about young children who get seriously ill, and how we can account for that. Can we hold them responsible for wreaking havoc in their own bodies? My answer is a qualified yes: first, the physical predetermination for a serious illness must be there as an accident or result of nature (this excludes congenital defects; no one can eradicate those). Second, the child himself may not be responsible, but I do think the child's environment may make him either give in to the physical predetermination, or not allow it to manifest itself, and, possibly, children who recover from a serious illness may have changed their environment with the illness so that it became tolerable. A man I know, who is older than I am, comes to mind here: he had leukemia when he was five and his family spoiled him ever since. Maybe he needed that extra attention to be able to live? I'm truly beginning to believe that illness, especially cancer, is never an "accident" in that the person who has it probably has something in his life that could be favorably affected by his having that illness, or the illness allows him to get out of some situation he doesn't want to be in. That's not saying the illness is any less real or serious, or that the mind can necessarily cure it, but that anyone confronted with such an illness would probably benefit from analyzing the changes in his life that might be considered a benefit from the disease, as well as the environment, internal or external, that may have helped allow the disease to take such a disastrous course. At least then he may have a measure of control over those aspects of the environment that can be changed, and if he makes the changes he will improve his life and chances of recovery.

The second discussion started when people were asking about how Mom is reacting to all of this. I told the story of the man who was showing her pictures of his granddaughter and how I thought she should express her feelings. The reaction against this was very strong, especially on the part of Linda, the woman whose 19-year-old daughter was killed in a hit-and-run accident. My point was that you can't allow people to comfort you if you don't let them know how you're feeling, and if they shy away from your feelings they are probably not worth having as friends.

Linda's counter point was that it doesn't do any good to make another person feel bad, because it only makes him avoid you and it doesn't make your pain go away – besides, people are simply not going to be sensitive all the time and it's not fair to embarrass them for being insensitive.

And yet I don't believe anyone has turned away from me when I've shared my feelings. Most people move closer, not further away. If I'm not trying to protect them, but just sharing my grief a little, they don't seem to turn away from that.

Am I wrong? Or am I just trying to teach the whole world when the world doesn't want to learn? What if I'd turned away from Kathy the first time she talked about her pregnancy when I got back to work? Wouldn't I feel my grief alone, and wouldn't she know she'd hurt me? And wouldn't that keep her from talking to me more and more in the fear of hurting me? I didn't turn away; I said it hurt and I said I enjoyed talking about it, too. I didn't want either of us to deny any part of our feelings – sad or happy I just wanted to acknowledge them.

I think our friendship deepened just <u>because</u> we were able to share the bad as well as the good; I think the friendship would never have evolved if I'd "saved" her from having to deal with my grief.

And that seems to be the way most people react. I really believe that when you think you're saving someone else's feelings, you're also trying to save your own, and instead of doing that, you – and the person whose feelings you are "saving", if he realizes it – are swallowing the emotion and end up carrying it around with you for a lot longer than if it were just brought out in the first place.

People seem to be afraid of honesty. They think it has to hurt. I don't think it has to hurt. I think it's possible to be honest and to share feelings without causing pain. You just have to listen carefully and be sensitive. And I guess you have to stop trying to teach the whole world.

I guess my whole gripe about the world as it is, is based on the fact that too many people refuse to take responsibility for their own lives: a drunk driver kills someone and he blames the bartender for not stopping him from drinking; a child is born with an abnormality, and the parents sue the doctor, as if a doctor could always know what could be wrong; a person gets cancer and blames the environment, a man never shares his feelings, dies stoically of a heart attack, and people admire him. Come on, people! Wake up! You can take charge of your own life. You are the only one who can do it for yourself. You need to share it with people who love you. Take credit when it's due you, and take responsibility when you're at fault. Feel your life, be a part of it! You don't know what's around the bend, so make the best of today, and make sure you can say to the highest authority "I did my best, and I'm proud of myself!" Are you listening, world?

Thursday, September 4, 1986

A.D. 39 weeks

6:45 a.m.

When I talk about being honest, I don't mean being cruel. For instance, going back to the man showing Mom pictures, maybe she could have said, "Did you see my granddaughter's pictures? I only have two, but they're very precious to me." Now the feelings are shared, and the man has a choice of response: "Oh. I'd like to see them," or "It makes me uncomfortable to see them." Now his feelings are out, too, and both can be accepted. Maybe I'm just asking for a perfect world.

Dave and I are honest with each other, and we hardly ever hurt each other with it. When we do hurt each other, we are usually well aware of it – we're not accidentally hurting each other's feelings with our honesty, we're purposely wording it so it hurts. That happens in many arguments, but on a day to day basis, our honesty does not hurt.

7:40 p.m.

Finally it's all over. My treatment this morning went well – I told the nurses that I would be happy to talk to groups or individuals that want to know more about the cancer.

Surgery was uncomfortable, as usual, but it went fast. In the recovery room I saw some people we knew – the wife was in for a biopsy of a breast lump which turned out to be benign.

Now I'm home, trying to drink ginger ale, but sacrificing it to the porcelain god intermittently. But I'm free! This is it! I can go on to make my dreams come true.

It's going to be hard to live with the knowledge that it could come back, but I'm not going to let that stop me from doing what I want. I will never say that cancer is the reason I won't do something I really want to do.

Tomorrow morning I can get up and take off the bandages and jump in the shower and not have to do any catheter care when I get out! If I get up the energy tonight I'm going to get rid of all the catheter paraphernalia in the room.

This is my last entry in this book. I said earlier that this is only a chapter in the book of my life. Cancer is not going to control my life, just be a part of it.

I'm tempted to give advice to readers at this point: whether you are ill or not, take charge of your life. Find reasons to be happy and make yourself happy. Nurture your friendships – they will strengthen if both of you are genuinely happy. You can be happy and sad at the same time: you must strive for that inner peace that true happiness and self-acceptance brings. Be aware of conflicts you are feeling so you can get them resolved as fast as possible, before they can start affecting your body. Remember, <u>you</u> make your diseases, you can help fight them by living a life that makes you genuinely happy. If you do get sick, <u>learn</u> from it.

I've gone through nine months of living with cancer now. Today is my rebirth: I start a new life today, cancer-free and healthy. My life has changed dramatically over these nine months, and mostly it's for the better. I have my inner peace, and my relationships with everyone are the best they've ever been. I have no regrets. The cancer didn't ruin my life.

A diagnosis of cancer doesn't necessarily mean a death sentence. It's possible to beat cancer with a good attitude and while continuing your daily activities.

But after nine months, I, for one, have had enough of it. I'm ready to jump into life head first. I think I'll start by making my beach dream come true.

292

THE END

EPILOGUE

I had completed this manuscript and added a happy ending in 1990: Three months after the end of chemotherapy, we conceived Ian Kirk Edwards (though not at the beach). He was born October 1, 1987 by Caesarian section because he was a week late and all of us were wary of taking any more chances with induced labor. I had an opportunity to change health plans so that Dr. Himes was still involved in my OB/GYN care. Ian started out blond and blue-eyed, although his hair darkened over time. It wasn't curly, but his baby brother, Erik David, born June 6, 1990, did have very blond curly hair and those same big blue peepers. Both boys were born big, strapping and healthy, and I was able to breastfeed them to my heart's content. I would have liked to have a vaginal delivery, but I was satisfied to have a healthy family. Our cat Cookie was also still with us. And Dave was definitely a great Daddy.

My brother married Leslie, whom he met in New York. The suit was settled out of court for $15,000 by his insurance company, and Hugo and Leslie moved to Florida. Their firstborn son, Derek, was born 8 days after Erik. Nicolette married Danny and they moved to Hawaii.

Dave's mother became ill with pancreatic cancer just before Ian's first birthday, and she died from it soon afterward. Everyone else in our families was still going strong.

I celebrated my 30th birthday a little suspiciously, as if I might reawaken the fates if I was too noisy! But I was starting to really believe that it was all behind me. I volunteered as a telephone counselor for Cancer Guidance Institute in Pittsburgh, a member of the National Coalition for Cancer Survivorship.

I did sell my article to *Ladies' Home Journal*, and from the letters and invitations to appear on television programs in response, my story touched many people.

Why then, did I put this manuscript away after only a few attempts at finding a publisher?

I think it was first of all, actually living the life I had been fighting for: a normal life with healthy children and a close, happy family. But it was also that I wondered if my story could actually make a difference. I was only two years in remission when I watched cancer take my mother-in-law. This really shook me.

Then, in 1992, when I had just barely achieved the magic five-year mark, my own mother was diagnosed with colon cancer.

Oh, she was a fighter! She already lived life joyfully and with gusto, and she kicked into high gear when she was diagnosed. She sought out every treatment: surgery, chemotherapy, shark fin powder, diet. She continued helping people in her psychotherapy practice, she traveled, she sailed, she camped, she bought a houseboat and tooled around on the river, she spent time with friends, she played with her grandsons (four by now, Ian, Erik, Derek, and little Jantje, named after my father Jan). She lit up the lives of everyone she touched.

But in the end, the cancer was too strong for her. In November of 1994, it was found in her liver, and she was told to put her affairs in order. Even then, she kept living life fully. We went skiing that winter, and she was faster down the slopes than I was. In the spring of 1995, the boys and I joined her and Dad on a cruise to the Caribbean. By then, she was pretty sick. She had been convinced to try one more experimental treatment: a catheter inserted in a vein in the groin, threaded up to the liver, and chemotherapy delivered straight to the tumors. This treatment robbed her of her energy, and also her hair, which she had been tenaciously holding on to throughout all of her previous treatments.

I begged her not to die on my birthday, May 15, and she complied, even ordering a gift from a catalog to arrive in time for my celebration. She told her friends not to come yet, to wait until the fall to see her. Then, on Memorial Day weekend, she slipped into a coma. Hugo and Nicolette and I took turns with Dad to stay by her bedside at home. She slipped away at 4 a.m. on June 4, 1995, with a little half-smile on her face as if she was still having a good time. She had just recently turned 56 years old. We buried her next to Gwynne and I imagine the two of them watching over me. Even 20 years later, I still mourn her deeply. I lost my best friend and biggest supporter.

I lost my will to share my story, because I felt like a fraud. My mother was the one who helped me deal with my cancer the most, and yet I had just watched her die from the same disease and could do nothing to help. What in the world could I have to offer?

Now, nearing the 30 year mark as a survivor, about to exceed the age my mother made it to, I can combine the lessons from my own and my mom's experience.

I recently watched a television show that shared Katie Couric's colonoscopy procedure. This was something my mom never got – her doctor didn't think it was necessary because she was in such excellent health. Had she had the recommended colonoscopy at 50, her cancer might have been found while she still had a fighting chance. According to the show, Katie Couric's courage to share the experience on live TV encouraged viewers to undergo the tests they needed for early diagnosis at the time their cancers were still very treatable. It also demystified the procedure and raised awareness of its benefits.

Maybe going back in history and sharing my roller coaster ride can have a similar effect on someone in the same way. It's not live television, but it sure is up close and personal.

One thing that I learned somewhere along the way was that there was a doctor in the early 1900's who tried to devise a cancer vaccine from a cocktail of different bacteria. He did this because he had a patient with recurrent sarcoma tumors in the neck, who spontaneously went into remission after he became ill with a bacterial infection. The infection was strep throat, or Group A Streptococcus. I had been infected with Group B Streptococcus – the bacteria that had been found in my uterus, placenta, and blood, and which had killed my daughter! I had to stay in the hospital an extra day to complete an intravenous antibiotic treatment to cure the infection. Could it be that this was what actually saved my life, not the surgery, radiation, and chemotherapy? Modern research in immunological treatments is showing some promise in this area.

I know that for myself, the cancer and the loss of my child changed my outlook on life. I focus on the positive, but I face the negative head on. I live by the "two-week rule": if I have a symptom that concerns me, I put a note in my calendar two weeks later to have it checked out. 95% of the time that date will come, and I will have completely forgotten about the symptom. That saves me two weeks of worry on a fairly regular basis. By the way, this does not apply to lumps. My experience has taught me that soft and malleable lumps are usually nothing, but if I discover anything in a breast or with a hard or immovable quality, I immediately make an appointment to have it checked out. But between the discovery and the appointment, the two-week rule applies.

The two-week rule is part of a strategy to minimize worry. Worry is a useless emotion. I'm not saying to "just stop" because that's impossible if you have a good reason for a concern. But the "what if's" just don't help. What's going to happen is going to happen, whether I've worried about it or not. I worried incessantly about my baby, and it had no effect on the disastrous outcome. I worried about dying young, and that hasn't happened – regardless of how much or little I worried about it. If I can use the two-week rule to suspend worry, I do. If I can take some sort of action and accept the consequences, then I do that. Does it look like my boss is getting ready to fire me? Go to a lawyer and find out how to navigate that process, get the resume updated and ready for shopping around, and start touching base with people in my network. Action displaces worry. If there's no action I can reasonably take, I resort to my mantra: "What I need will come to me when I need it." So often I have repeated that to myself and the same day received something to meet my need – a phone call asking if I'd be interested in a job interview, an unexpected refund check that helps cover the bills, an encouraging visit from an old friend during a down moment.

And if all else fails, I remember the comment made by one of my favorite bosses, who had a remarkable ability to see trouble coming and find a way around it: "I tried worrying once. I didn't like it."

I take care of myself. I do my best to balance my life. People tell me I eat healthy. By that I mean, I do it out of habit, and people notice and point it out, but I'm not on a soapbox telling them that I do it. I developed a passion for rowing when I turned 40, and now I belong to a competitive team that travels to races. This has a double benefit – it keeps me fit and it gives me a large group of friends to round out my social life and support network.

When I encounter people who are dealing with cancer or grief, I share my experience with them, but paying attention to how they are taking it. Sometimes I only tell them a little bit and then give them my contact information and encourage them to contact me any time if they need to talk. I especially encourage them to talk to me about the stuff their loved ones don't want to hear – the fears, the anger, the resentment, or just the details of how the treatments feel. If they do ask questions, I answer openly and honestly, and completely. Sometimes, though, I know it's enough just to know that someone has survived. When I was being wheeled in for my first C-section a nurse said to me, "I see you have sarcoma. I had that 25 years ago. Does that help?" Oh, yes, it certainly did.

I go to funerals. They are for those left behind, and our support at their time of loss speaks volumes. I still remember all those people in the cemetery on that bright day witnessing that tiny coffin. I felt so blessed to have all of them there supporting me. I try to pay that forward.

From my parents I learned to embrace adventures and treat people with respect, humor, and thoughtfulness. I remember following my dad through a dodgy neighborhood in Mexico, and him walking up to people, looking them in the eye, shaking their hand, sharing a laugh, and leaving behind another friend.

At one time I attended a leadership seminar that talked about positive focus. "You get what you focus on," was the lesson. I was not really buying it until the workshop leader told this story. She was skydiving and in mid-air realized she was not going to make her target. Below her she saw acres and acres of prairie land and one little line across it. That little line was a barbed wire fence. "I don't want to land on that fence!" was all she could think. Guess where she landed? On the thing she was focused on – the fence. Our subconscious doesn't recognize "don't", just the thing receiving the focus. All she had to do was shift her focus to "I do want to land in that big open space over there." I've found that focusing on what I don't want only gets me that. Focusing on what I do want doesn't necessarily get it handed to me (I don't think the Universe will give me exactly what I want), but it does leave me open to recognizing an opportunity to make the thing I want happen.

I believe that was what I was doing by refusing to accept advice to leave in the catheter, keep in mind that it might come back, save 50 days' worth of Heparin, or wait for five years before becoming pregnant again. If I had done any of those things, I would have been focusing on the cancer and its possible return. I focused on the life I wanted, and did everything to make that happen. Even if I would not have succeeded completely, at least I would have enjoyed the time I had more – just like my mom did with her limited time.

I'll never know whether it was the surgery, the chemotherapy, the radiation, the strep infection, the hypnosis, all the self-reflection, my attitude, my support network, my sense of humor, or some combination of the above that saved my life. I do know that I like the person I became as a result of the experience.

What I want now is to live a life that honors my mother. She helped people every day, and she managed a balance between all the areas of her life. She gave love, she listened, she soothed, she cheered, she ran outside on beautiful spring days to play tennis or sail or ride horses (or all three if she could manage it), she spent rainy days relaxed on the couch with a good book, she traveled, she loved to watch car chases on TV, she told silly jokes, she loved animals, she mediated, she made peace, she had a glass of wine with my dad, she hugged everybody, she watched sunsets, she dragged people's life stories out of them with her endless questions, she sewed artistic quilts, she remodeled, she impressed colleagues with her quiet competence, she socialized, she made delicious holiday meals, she sat quietly smiling at her daughter over a cup of tea. Her absence left a big hole in a lot of people's hearts.

It looks like I'm going to get the years she didn't get to experience, so I intend to make the very best use of them that I can. I'm excited to experience whatever life has to offer next, and joyful to be alive to experience it.

TO MY MOTHER

Marijke Mathilde van Linden van den Heuvell-Stades
4/17/1939 – 6/4/1995

Like an angel on earth you embraced us

your warmth calmed us

your love sustained us

your praise buoyed us

your joy uplifted us

your kindness healed us

your understanding mellowed us

your acceptance cherished us

your faith strengthened us

I miss you so

Now I can only see you in my mind's eye:

the glow of a fire on a distant shore

I reach out for your comfort, too far away,

and long to feel your warmth once more

My tears distort the glow I see,

reveal tiny meandering embers

and one of them is me

Can I nurture that spark of you

in me?

If in faith I glow with warmth,

sigh praise and leap for joy,

spread love,

accept, understand, embrace,

can our light bathe the ones

I touch?

Can I kindle your spark to live in me?